ERNEST HEMINGWAY
IN THE *Yellowstone High Country*

A Complete Account of Hemingway's Work and Adventures in Montana and Wyoming

Fight the fight!
Enjoy the Adventure!
Chris Warren

CHRIS WARREN

RIVERBEND
PUBLISHING

Ernest Hemingway in the Yellowstone High Country
Copyright © 2019 by Chris Warren

Published by Riverbend Publishing, Helena, Montana

ISBN 13: 978-1-60639-114-3

Printed in the United States of America.

2 3 4 5 6 7 8 9 0 VP 25 24 23 22 21 20 19

Cataloging-in-Publication data is on file at the Library of Congress.

Cover and text design by Sarah Cauble, www.sarahcauble.com

Riverbend Publishing
P.O. Box 5833
Helena, MT 59604
1-866-787-2363
www.riverbendpublishing.com

Cover photo: Ernest Hemingway on a hunting trip in the Yellowstone High Country near Cooke City, Montana, in 1930.
PATRICK HEMINGWAY PAPERS, C0066, MANUSCRIPTS DIVISION, DEPARTMENT OF RARE BOOKS AND SPECIAL COLLECTIONS, PRINCETON UNIVERSITY LIBRARY.

Back cover photos:
ERNEST HEMINGWAY COLLECTION. JOHN F. KENNEDY PRESIDENTIAL LIBRARY AND MUSEUM, BOSTON.

Dedicated to the memory of

"Walkin'" Tom Weaver of Red Lodge

and

Greg "the leg" Watson of Cooke City

Acknowledgments

I would first like to thank my publisher, Chris Cauble and everyone at Riverbend Publishing for their faith in a first-time author. Next I would like to pay tribute to the Lewis-Reynolds-Smith Founders Fellowship and their sponsorship of Hemingway scholarship, independent and otherwise, especially Debra Moddlemog and Verna Kale. Also, a nod to libraries in general and to three in particular: the Wyoming Room at Sheridan County Fulmer Public Library, the Ernest Hemingway Collection at the John F. Kennedy Presidential Library and Museum, and the Patrick Hemingway Collection at the Firestone Library, Princeton University.

I am especially indebted to this group of Hemingway aficionados and local historians: George McCormick, Tom Weaver, Ralph Glidden, Dink Bruce, Kay King, Larry Grimes, Stephen Brown, and Phil Greene. Also, Raz and Maddie Schneider, Josh Snider, Brian Boyle, Patrick Hemingway, Nick and Molly Levy, Rick Porter, Adam Skaggs, Mike Flynn, Jay Kirby, G. Kimball Hart, Sue Hart, Judy Slack, Kim Ostermeyer, John Sutton, Debi Isaakson, Shannon Smith, Jeff Snider, Alix House, Henry Finkbeiner, Bill Blackford, Jon Fryer, Danny Eaton, Kim Ostermeyer, Christine Buyse, and everyone at the Miners Saloon and Beartooth Café in Cooke City and the Uptown Billiards Club in Portland. And finally thank you to Patty Ma, Edna Warren, Jacque Warren, and Miles and Sophia who are my inspiration and motivation.

Contents

Introduction

Cooke City, Montana, is a town unlike any other in the United States. It sits nestled among the rugged peaks of the Beartooth Mountains, just outside of Yellowstone National Park's northeast boundary. The year-round population is around a hundred; there is no hospital, no high school, no grocery store, and no police. The nearest traffic light is two hours away. At 7,800 feet in elevation, Cooke City averages more than 200 inches of snow a year.

Despite this seclusion, there has always been a cosmopolitan feel to the small town. Proximity to Yellowstone has brought people here from all over the world. Since the first accounts of Yellowstone's smoldering landscape made it back east, people have come to this out-of-the-way spot for their own reasons: gold, furs, land, solitude, wilderness, adventure, or even as a place to lay low for a while. These days they come for Yellowstone, wolves, trout, elk, snow, wilderness, adventure, or as a place to lay low for a while.

Why would Ernest Hemingway, the twentieth century's most iconic author, name Cooke City as one of his favorite places to write in the world? How could a town this small and remote end up on a list with such literary hotspots as Madrid and Paris, and Hemingway-ville itself, Key West?

After my first couple of years working and living in Cooke City, I attended the University of Montana and took a course on Hemingway. His 1938 book, *The First Forty-nine Stories*, was on the syllabus, and as I picked my way through the stories, I came across a line in the preface that mentioned Cooke City as a great place to write. I was shocked.

When I returned to Cooke (as locals often abbreviate the name) the following summer, I asked about Hemingway but found very little information and
even less interest. That is, until I met Ralph Glidden, the owner of the Cooke
City General Store. Ralph had moved to Cooke in the early 1970s and had
been intrigued by Hemingway's connection to the area. At that time there
were still some people who remembered Hemingway's visits. Olive Nordquist,
who had known Hemingway and still resided in Cooke, hired Ralph to help
run her hotel. In the 1930s Olive and her husband had run the nearby L—T
(pronounced "L Bar T") guest ranch on the Clark's Fork during Hemingway's
first three visits there and even went to see him in Key West. She was very fond
of the Hemingway family and happy to share her memories of them. Ralph
had also known a few of the caretakers at other ranches in the Clark's Fork
Valley and through them had learned much of the history of Hemingway's
time in the area.[1]

A few years later I met another character who would go on to become a
great friend and a big help with my research. Tom Weaver was having a beer at
the Miners Saloon in Cooke City. He was hard to miss, well over six-feet-tall
with a white beard and sporting a beret. Tom was from Red Lodge, Montana,
another small town on the other side of the Beartooth Mountains from Cooke
City, and a published writer himself. He told me that his father had been a
friend of Hemingway during the writer's time in the mountains.

The next summer my wife and I opened a coffee shop in Cooke City and
Tom came to visit. He gave me a copy of the recently published *True at
First Light*, Hemingway's memoir of his second and final trip to Africa. Tom
had dog-eared a couple of pages where Cooke City and the Beartooth Pass
were mentioned. After reading the novel, I realized that after twenty years,
two marriages, a world war, a Nobel Prize, and while living on another continent, Hemingway's mind still drifted back to his time in the Yellowstone
High Country.[2]

Soon after the publication of *True at First Light*, I came across an article in
the 2006 Fly Fishing edition of *Big Sky Journal* about Hemingway's first summer in the Beartooths. From the article I learned that Hemingway had spent

time in Hoosiers Bar, which not only was still operating in Cooke City but was the chief sponsor of our local softball team. The article also shed light on Tom Weaver's connection to Hemingway, revealing that he was the son of Chub Weaver, who is immortalized in Hemingway's greatest novel, *For Whom the Bell Tolls*, as one of Hemingway's best friends.[3]

At this point I realized that I had met two people (Ralph and Tom) whose generosity and enthusiasm had kept alive my interest in Hemingway until I had found direct connections between the Yellowstone area and Hemingway's work. It was then I decided to try and make something cohesive out of the information I was finding.

My project began in earnest when I read Carlos Baker's comprehensive biography, *Ernest Hemingway: A Life Story.* From this book I was able to discern exactly when the author was here and with whom he came. I then acquired two books of Hemingway letters: *Selected Letters,* also by Carlos Baker, and *The Only Thing That Counts*, a collection of letters exchanged between Hemingway and his editor Max Perkins. By cross-referencing the dates when he was at the ranch with the dates on the letters, I was able to get a good idea of what Hemingway's life in the Yellowstone High Country had been like.

In *Selected Letters* are many letters Hemingway wrote to friends imploring them to join him here, and long accounts of his days hunting and fishing. In *The Only Thing That Counts*, there was a record of the writing he did here. In these letters I found many references to Cooke City and Red Lodge, as well as to many of the mountains, lakes, and rivers that were already familiar to me.

The biography and letters also shed light on a Hemingway I never knew existed: a family man who fished with his wife and taught his children to fish and ride horses. A man who joined in the kids' baseball games in a horse corral, and who told ghost stories around campfires while wearing a goofy hat. A man who could at one moment eruditely entertain his wife's wealthy friends and the next moment ride a horse into some of the world's most rugged backcountry. He was also a man burdened by the implications left him by his father's suicide. Where was the media construct of the drunken, womanizing, egomaniac with the big white beard and cable-knit sweater?

Next I began reading all of Hemingway's work. I found connections to the Beartooths, Cooke City, and the ranch in seven novels, several short stories, a half dozen articles, and countless letters. When I read the story "A Man of the World," I realized that I had come across something special. The story is quite obviously set in Cooke City, but Hemingway had named it Jessup. After doing a little research, I found that "A Man of the World" was the last work that Ernest Hemingway had published in his lifetime. It was published in the 100th anniversary issue of *The Atlantic Monthly*[4] in December 1957, and it was essentially dismissed by critics as an ugly little story not worthy of the author's legacy. The little criticism that exists of this story fails to connect it to Cooke City and to Hemingway's five summers spent on the ranch ten miles east of there. (Appendix IV examines this story and these connections in detail.)

For Whom the Bell Tolls also revealed the importance of the Yellowstone High Country. The protagonist, Robert Jordan, hails from Red Lodge and all of his memories and flashbacks are based on Hemingway's time at the ranch. In particular, I knew from Baker's biography that Hemingway's father had shot himself with his father's Civil War-era Smith and Wesson revolver, and that Hemingway's mother had sent the gun to Hemingway just before his first trip to the Yellowstone area. From Tom Weaver I knew that Hemingway and Tom's father, Chub, had ridden regularly from Red Lodge to the ranch, and on one of those trips, Hemingway rid himself of the gun by dropping it into a deep mountain lake. In *For Whom the Bell Tolls*, while trying to drum up the courage to blow up the bridge, Jordan struggles with the memory of his father's suicide and recounts dropping his father's gun into a mountain lake, even mentioning his riding partner, Chub, by name. It was then I realized that events in the Yellowstone High Country had major significance to both Hemingway's work and his life.[9]

At this point I knew the exact dates of Hemingway's visits, but my resources were limited and at the time, internet in Cooke City was painfully slow. So any time I traveled to a city—mostly Missoula and Bozeman, Montana, and Portland, Oregon—I would head to bookstores and libraries to do research.

I would search indexes for any reference to Hemingway's time in the Yellowstone High Country. Whenever I found something of value I would either buy the book or scribble down the important information and log it into my computer the first chance I got.

The question now was why hadn't all this information been brought to light? Ernest Hemingway's life and work has been dissected and analyzed, perhaps, more than any other American writer. It seemed impossible that there could be a gap in the story. Even though Hemingway sent off final drafts of major works from the Cooke City General Store and Post Office, there was not even a plaque or a sign in the town.[10]

As I continued my research there were highs and lows, times when I thought I was the sole possessor of some crucial piece of information only to find an article that had made the same discovery several years earlier. As I kept on digging I began to realize why the contributions of this little corner of the world to the life and work of Hemingway had been so under-examined and undervalued. The L—T Ranch sits in Wyoming, while Cooke City resides ten miles away in Montana. Robert Jordan is from Red Lodge; the short story "The Gambler, the Nun and the Radio" takes place in Billings, Montana; Thomas Hudson from *Islands in the Stream* owns a ranch in Montana. In the *Green Hills of Africa,* Hemingway refers to hunting Timber Creek, a small creek near the ranch that is twenty miles from any road. In *True at First Light* Hemingway remembers hunting in Wyoming. "A Man of the World" is set in Cooke City, but it is called Jessup.

To the south of the L—T Ranch are the Absaroka Mountains, to the north are the Beartooth Mountains, and to the west is Yellowstone National Park. In short, the location of the ranch and Hemingway's use of so many descriptions had created an ambiguity that made it virtually impossible to combine all the literary and biographical clues. I realized that if you didn't have knowledge of his life and work and a close understanding of the terrain, you probably could not make the connections. The fact that in more than fifty years no one had linked his last published work to Cooke City is a testament to this blind spot in the scholarship.

To help fill in the blanks, I set about trying to find people's personal recollections of the famous writer when he was here. Ralph Glidden again proved instrumental. Ralph sent me copies of articles written in 1970 upon the publication of *Islands in the Stream*.[12] The authors of the articles had interviewed several people who had known Hemingway during his stays at the ranch, so now I had several first-person accounts of Hemingway's time in the area. From these accounts I realized two things: one, the people who knew the Hemingways best, Chub Weaver, Ivan Wallace, the Nordquists, and Polly Copeland, all had very positive impressions of the man and his family. And two, there was a tendency for people to embellish their accounts. Because it had been thirty to forty years since their lives had crossed, people sometimes just added their own twist to the tale.

One resident of the Spear-O-Wigwam Ranch in the Bighorn Mountains remembered "Ernie" telling her that his favorite places in the world were Wyoming and Africa.[13] Well, Hemingway was at her ranch in 1928, but he would not set foot on the African continent for another five years. Another source suggested that "Wine of Wyoming" was inspired by his time on the Clark's Fork,[14] when in reality that story was published before Hemingway's first trip to the Clark's Fork Valley. Even Hemingway's two most respected biographers, Carlos Baker and Michael Reynolds, differ on his initial arrival at the L—T Ranch. Baker had him first stopping at a ranch on Sunlight Creek in Wyoming before finding his way to the L—T, meaning he would have come from the east.[15] Reynolds had Hemingway traveling to the ranch through Yellowstone National Park and Cooke City, meaning he would have come from the west.[16] So even before my story could begin, I had to sort out which version was true. I turned to local history and an eyewitness account of the Hemingway's arrival from Polly Copeland: "[Hemingway's car] was the first automobile that ever dared to travel the perilous horse trail, traversing the roaring Clark's Fork at intervals from Crandall on." Problem solved: he came from the east.[17]

I realized that for my project to have any legitimacy, I would have to be very careful about what I included. Also, since this is a work of non-fiction, I had to be very careful to not fall into the same traps myself. I could not fill in gaps with my own assumptions; everything I included would have to be verified and cited. Rather than just paraphrasing other peoples' work, I decided to quote and give full credit rather than risk unintentional plagiarism. As I began to compile all of this information, I realized that the story of Hemingway's time in the Yellowstone High Country had a beginning, middle, and end, that it had conflict and resolution, and that it was pertinent to both his work and biography and to the history of the area.

The story began with the birth of his second son, the beginning of his second marriage, the completion of *A Farewell to Arms*, his first trip out west, and the death of his father. It ended with the end of his second marriage, the beginning of the deterioration of his relationship with his sons, the Spanish Civil War and the onset of World War II, and the completion of *For Whom the Bell Tolls*. In between there were three other novels, his first trip to Africa, the Great Depression, and many of his best short stories. There was the best big game hunting of his life outside of Africa, including black bear, grizzly bear, elk, deer, and bighorn sheep, and what he considered the best trout fishing of his life.[18]

At this point I was feeling pretty good about the project when my wife, Patty, met a man at the Miners Saloon (again), who would prove invaluable to the project. Dink Bruce winters in Key West and summers in Livingston, Montana, and moves comfortably through the literary circles there.[20] Dink was at the Miners with Jon Fryer, owner of the venerable Sax and Fryer Bookstore in Livingston. Patty struck up a conversation, and eventually my project came up. That was when Dink revealed that his father, Otto Bruce, had been Hemingway's long-time friend and driver.[19]

The men were very supportive and gracious, and two weeks later, to my astonishment, a couple arrived at our coffee shop with a manila envelope containing pictures from Dink's personal collection. The pictures were stunning: here was Ernest Hemingway as a young man, rifle slung over his shoulder, here he was with Pauline and their fishing rods, Hemingway with his bighorn sheep, and pictures of his sons with bear hides. Once again a local resident with personal memories and knowledge of Hemingway's time here had come into our lives and generously contributed to the project by offering enthusiasm, support, and, this time, his own photographs of the Hemingway family.

I needed to take one more step and approach Hemingway's estate and family. I was very nervous as I had heard they were quite sensitive about any exploitation of the Hemingway legacy. When I met Patrick Hemingway at a library fundraiser in Bozeman, I was immediately put at ease. Patrick, at 86, was gracious and encouraging, and when I told him that I had lived in Cooke City for the past 23 years and had raised a family there, he was instantly supportive of my project. We talked about Chub Weaver and about how Cooke City and the ranch had not changed much over the years. Patrick also agreed with me that there was a gap in the scholarship when it came to his father's time in the Yellowstone High Country. He was not interested in approving my work and told me it was my interpretation that mattered. After encouraging me to drop his name when asking for permission to publish, I left with greater confidence that my work could make a positive impact on the Hemingway world. My research has convinced me that these mountains that I call home, and the wildness that resides within them, had an undeniable impact on both the life and work of one of the most influential writers of the twentieth century.

In naming this region, I have referred to Ralph Glidden's book *Exploring the Yellowstone High Country: A History of the Cooke City Area,* and decided to borrow a phrase from his title.[11] What follows is a complete account of Ernest Hemingway's time in the Yellowstone High Country.

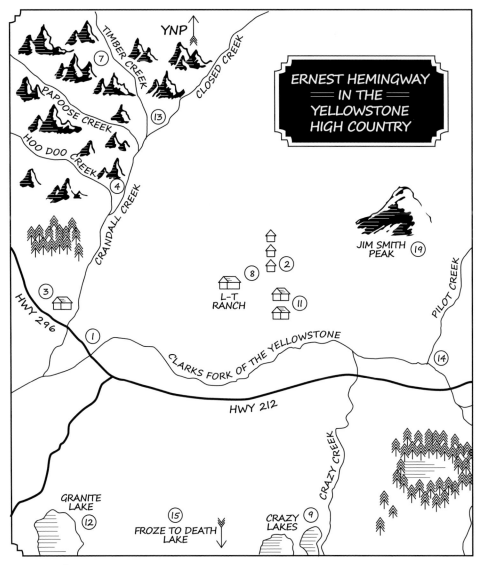

MAP KEY

1. 1930, Hemingway becomes the first person to cross the Clark's Fork in a car. (History of Ranches, Spencer)

2. 1930, Wrote 350 pages of *Death in the Afternoon* in cabin 1 of the L-T ranch. (Letter to Perkins 8-12-30)

3. Crandall Ranger Station, Hemingway stopped here after gashing his chin and knee, borrowed car to get to Cody. (Baker p. 274)

4. Returns from Cody with stitches in his face and whiskey in his gut and shoots first bear. (Baker p. 274)

5. Hemingway shoots the only bighorn sheep of his life on the slopes of Pilot and Index peaks. (*Vogue*, February 1939)

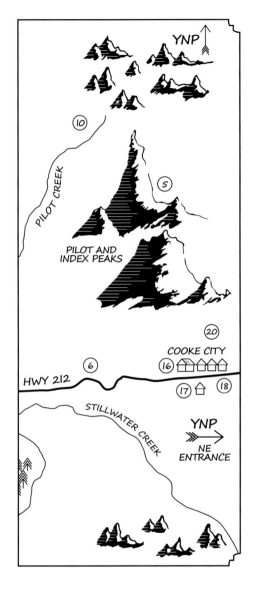

8. "The Light of the World" written here in August 1932. (Reynolds p. 97)

9. The Hemingway and Murphy families go on a camping and fishing trip to the Crazy Lakes, 1932. (Baker p. 297)

10. Hemingway shoots a "hell of a big [black] bear" in October 1932. (Letter to Strater 10-14-32)

11. *To Have and Have Not* written here in 1936. (Letter to Arnold Gingrich 9-16-36)

12. Spent three days hunting and fishing with Tommy and Lorraine Shevlin at Granite Lake in 1936, catching "6 over 16 inch (rainbows) 4 over 18 inch." (Letter to Gingrich 9-16-36)

13. Hemingway hunts with Shevlins up Timber Creek, shooting elk and grizzly bears. (Letter to A. MacLeish 9-26-36

14. Road builders searching for gravel for the Beartooth Highway ruin Hemingway's favorite fishing spot, the confluence of Pilot Creek and the Clark's Fork. (Baker p. 296)

15. On a pack trip over the Beartooth Mountains, Hemingway drops his grandfather's Smith and Wesson revolver into the deep cold waters of Froze-to-Death Lake. This episode and its significance are described in *For Whom the Bell Tolls,* some of which was written at the ranch. (Chap. 30)

16. The Cooke City General Store: manuscripts, short stories, and countless letters were sent from here in the 1930s, and the store is mentioned in *True at First Light.* (Baker and letters)

17. Hoosiers Bar opened in 1934. When Hemingway went to Hoosiers in 1936, 1938 and 1939, the bar was open all night much like the fictional "Index" bar in "A Man of the World." (*Big Sky Journal*-Fall 2006)

18. Hemingway and his wife never missed a Saturday night in 1938 and 1939 at the Gorham Chalet (now the Range Rider). (*Village Boy*, Ralph Nelles)

19. Jim Smith was the original owner the of L—T Ranch. His 1912 murder was a source of inspiration for Hemingway in "The Snows of Kilimanjaro."

20. Cooke City (renamed "Jessup" by Hemingway) is the setting for "A Man of the World," Hemingway's final published story. (*Atlantic Monthly*, 100th anniversary issue)

6. After hunting sage grouse and enjoying what he called the "finest shooting ever in my life," Hemingway's Model A Ford hit a rock and started leaking oil, forcing him to "coast 4 miles back to Cooke" to get it fixed. (Letter to Perkins 8-8-32)

7. Hemingway shot a 7-point bull elk at almost 11,000-feet in elevation here. (Letter to H. Strater 10-14-32)

The Players

Ernest Hemingway

It has been suggested that there were only two kinds of writers in the twentieth century: those who tried to write like Hemingway and those who tried not to. Such was his influence on modern literature. His ability to convey complex ideas and emotions using direct and simple language impressed critics and, at the same time, invited ordinary Americans into his world.

Born at the end of the 1800s, Hemingway grew up listening to his grandfather's stories of the Civil War. At the time of Hemingway's death in 1961, he had been involved in World Wars I and II and the Spanish Civil War, witnessed the dropping of the atomic bomb, and watched the birth of the space race.

Hemingway never went to college, instead volunteering to serve as an ambulance driver in WWI. He became the first American wounded on the Italian front, suffering 227 shrapnel wounds during a mortar attack. After the war Hemingway moved to Paris where he lived with his new wife, Hadley Richardson, and their son Jack, or "Bumby" as he was affectionately known. The Hemingways fell in with a literary crowd of ex-pats that included Gertrude Stein and F. Scott Fitzgerald, becoming part of what would later be called the "Lost Generation." In 1927 Hemingway left Hadley for Pauline Pfeiffer. The couple had two boys, Patrick and Gregory.

As the Roaring Twenties gave way to the Great Depression, Hemingway entered the most successful and prolific part of his career. Between 1925 and

1940 he published four collections of stories, five novels, two works of non-fiction, a play, a film, and countless articles and correspondences.

It was during this period that Hemingway became known as a world-class sportsman, catching marlin, sailfish, and tuna in the Caribbean, bagging wild trout in the rivers of America, and chasing big game in the Rocky Mountains and across Africa. His house on Whitehead Street in Key West served as his winter home, while a log cabin at the L—T Ranch near the Montana-Wyoming border was his summer home.

Hemingway interrupted this comfortable and productive arrangement to report on the Spanish Civil War. During this conflict he started a stormy, war-torn romance with another war correspondent, Martha Gellhorn. Leaving Pauline for Martha cost Hemingway the home in Key West, his retreat in the mountains, and many of his friends. He moved his residences to Cuba and Sun Valley, Idaho. His marriage to Gellhorn would last only as long as World War II. As the war ended, Hemingway married Mary Welsh; she would be his lover, companion, and eventual caretaker.

After World War II, Hemingway published *Across the River and into the Trees* and the Pulitzer Prize-winning novella *The Old Man and the Sea.* He also wrote *The Garden of Eden, Islands in the Stream,* and articles that would become *The Dangerous Summer,* all of which were published posthumously. He made another hunting trip to Africa (where he survived two plane crashes), and he was awarded the Nobel Prize for Literature in 1954.

In his later years, Hemingway descended into alcoholism and depression, leading to electro-shock therapy at the Mayo Clinic. On July 2, 1961, like his father, his first wife's father, his only brother, one of his sisters, and later a granddaughter, Ernest Hemingway killed himself.

Pauline Pfeiffer Hemingway

Pauline Pfeiffer was Hemingway's second wife and mother of his two youngest sons. Their marriage coincided with Hemingway's time in the Yellowstone High Country. Pauline was with Ernest for all five summers he spent at the

L—T Ranch in the Clark's Fork Valley. She quickly became popular with everyone at the ranch. She had her own 28 gauge shotgun and her own fly rod. After picking wild berries, Pauline would mix them with gin and powdered sugar to make a powerful cocktail. Their marriage ended during Hemingway's final summer at the ranch.

Jack (Bumby), Patrick, and Gregory Hemingway

The three boys were a constant at the ranch, learning to fish and ride horses. As adults, all three have said they considered their times in the Clark's Fork Valley as some of their happiest. Jack learned to fish on the Clark's Fork and would later write *The Misadventures of a Fly Fisherman*. Patrick was with his father on a famous bear hunt in 1936. His godfather, Chub Weaver, taught him to read on that trip. Gregory was at the ranch in 1939, enjoying what he considered to be some of his happiest times with his father. Two of the three boys, Patrick and Gregory, eventually settled in Montana.

Lawrence Nordquist

Lawrence Nordquist was the proprietor and owner of the L—T Ranch where Hemingway stayed five times from 1930 to 1939. The letters "L" and "T" in the ranch name stood for the first and last letters in his name. He was married to Olive Nordquist for Ernest and Pauline's first three visits, and the two couples became very close, going on camping and fishing trips of a week or more. The Nordquists even visited the Hemingways in Key West. After separating from Olive and giving up his interest in the ranch, Lawrence moved to Cooke City, building what is now the Beartooth Café.

Olive Nordquist

Olive was very fond of the Hemingways, spending the summers with them at the L—T in 1930, 1932, and 1936, and visiting them in Key West in the winter of 1931. After her divorce from Lawrence, Olive moved to Cooke City and operated the Nordquist Cabins at the east end of town. She remained in Cooke City until 1989 and was one of the last people in the area to have direct knowledge of the Hemingways. She provided much information to Hemingway biographers and to Hemingway fans passing through.

Leland Stanford (Chub) Weaver

Chub Weaver was Hemingway's best friend in the area. Chub was from Red Lodge, Montana, and worked at the L—T during the 1930s as a hunting and fishing guide. His friendship with Hemingway lasted until the writer's death. Chub was one of the few people Hemingway called after his final trip to the Mayo Clinic. The two men not only hunted and fished together but they also drank together, took road trips, and were both world travelers and family men. Weaver was godfather to Hemingway's second son Patrick, even teaching him to read on a grizzly bear hunt in 1936. Chub was with Hemingway on a horseback trip over the Beartooth Mountains when Hemingway dropped his grandfather's gun into Froze-to-Death Lake. The two men had discussed suicide, and Chub was not surprised when he got the news from Sun Valley. Toward the end of *For Whom the Bell Tolls*, Hemingway paid tribute to this friendship by including Chub in a list of the main character's closest friends.

John Staebe

Spelled "Staib" in *Green Hills of Africa*, Staebe was a mountain man in the Yellowstone area in the 1930s and 1940s. His experiences in Germany during WWI had left him deaf, but he was well respected as a man of the woods. Staebe and Hemingway had WWI and love for mountains in common. In *Green Hills of Africa,* Hemingway talks of sharing some of the habits of African guides with Staebe. His loss of hearing and how he dealt with it was the type of attribute Hemingway admired most in men. The author suffered through a rash of serious injuries during his time in the high country and many of the fictional characters he created during that time were people who had stoically endured their injuries and maintained their integrity while doing so. The real-life Staebe would have fit right in with those characters. In an eerie coincidence, Staebe took his own life in 1953. When he felt he could no longer take care of himself, he wrote a note apologizing for not digging his own grave in the frozen ground, shot his horses, and then himself.

Ivan Wallace, the Allington brothers, and Huck Mees—the ranch hands

Ivan Wallace was close to Hemingway during the 1930 and 1932 visits and gave a couple of interviews in 1970 about their time together. The Allington brothers were in charge of bringing liquor and wine over the mountains from Red Lodge to the L—T. Floyd Allington was on his way to Key West with Hemingway and writer John Dos Passos when Hemingway broke his writing arm in a car accident. Huck Mees was another legendary mountain man around the ranch. In 1931 Mees became the first person to climb Pilot Peak. He would join Hemingway on a black bear hunt up Pilot Creek the following year.

Maxwell "Max" Perkins

Perkins was Hemingway's editor at Charles Scribner's Sons until his death in 1946. Perkins never visited the ranch but maintained contact with Hemingway while he was in the mountains. They exchanged drafts of *To Have and Have Not, Death in the Afternoon,* and *The First Forty-nine Stories* by mail, and the editor gradually accepted the value of the Yellowstone High Country to his most important client. Perkins was the only person that exchanged letters with Hemingway every time he headed west, and those letters offer the ultimate insight into the work Hemingway did over those six seasons.

Other visitors to the ranch

Bill Horne

A friend of Hemingway since his time in Italy during WWI, Horne accompanied Hemingway on his trip to Wyoming's Bighorn Mountains in 1928, where he met "Bunny," his future wife. Bill and Bunny visited Hemingway at the L—T in 1930 and enjoyed some epic fishing. The couple returned to the ranch the following year when the Hemingways weren't there and contributed to a letter penned by folks at the ranch to Ernest and Pauline.

John Dos Passos

Dos Passos was an American writer and friend of Hemingway for twenty years. He visited Hemingway at the ranch in 1930 and traveled the high country with Hemingway, Chub, Ivan Wallace, and Nordquist. At the end of that summer he drove from the ranch with Hemingway and Floyd Allington. Although Dos Passos and Hemingway worked alongside each other as war correspondents during the Spanish Civil War, their relationship began to deteriorate as their political views diverged. Dos Passos also resented his likeness to the Richard Gordon character in *To Have and Have Not. By* the time of Hemingway's final visit to the ranch in 1939, his friendship with Dos Passos was essentially over.

Gerald and Sara Murphy

The Murphys had been friends with Ernest and Pauline since their days together in Paris. They visited the Hemingways in the summer of 1932, taking trips to the Crazy Lakes and Pilot Creek. A high society couple, they objected to the lack of a good chef at the ranch and complained about being served canned fruit cocktail in the backcountry. In her memoir, their daughter Honoria Murphy Donelly fondly remembered her time with Hemingway, stating that of all of her parents' friends, it was Hemingway who genuinely seemed interested in her and her siblings.

Charles Thompson

One of Hemingway's closest friends, the Key West native was one of the men who taught Hemingway to fish the big water of the Gulf Stream. In return, Hemingway introduced Thompson to the big game opportunities of the Yellowstone High Country in 1932. The following year the two men traveled to Africa to hunt that continent's game. Thompson was part of a powerful Key West family that included a sheriff and a county commissioner; there is still a statue of his brother Norberg on the harbor walk, near the Mel Fisher Museum.

Tommy and Lorraine Shevlin

The Shevlins visited Hemingway in Key West in the spring of 1936, and they came to the ranch that summer. The Shevlins were with Hemingway when he shot his only grizzly bear. Shevlin shot a bigger bear than his host, then beat him in an ensuing horse race and crap game, and went on to pan *To Have and Have Not*, which caused Hemingway to angrily throw the manuscript out of his cabin window. Hemingway would suggest later that Lorraine Shevlin had been an inspiration for Margot Macomber in the short story, "The Short Happy Life of Francis Macomber."

The Ford Car

The Ford that Ernest, Pauline, and Bumby drove to the ranch that first summer seems to have been a character in itself. Described upon arrival by Polly Copeland as "an old, travel worn Model T, 'tin-lizzy,' with an ax and shovel slung along the side," it was actually a 1928 Ford Model A Roadster Coupe. Later it was shipped across the Atlantic and made some famous runs from Paris to the bullfights in Pamplona, Spain. In 1928, after the birth of Patrick Hemingway, Ernest used the car to drive to Sheridan, Wyoming, and the Cloud Peak area. After finishing *A Farewell to Arms,* he drove around the countryside with western writer Owen Wister and shot prairie dogs from the Ford's windows. The "tin lizzy" entered Clark's Fork Valley folklore when, in 1930, it became the first car to cross the Clark's Fork River.

In a 1932 letter from the ranch, Hemingway mentions taking the car to shoot grouse, then busting the oil pan and "coasting" four miles downhill to Cooke City. After an eventful summer, Hemingway then headed out of the high country with Dos Passos and Floyd Allington, through Cooke City, spending the night within earshot of a gurgling geyser at Mammoth Hot Springs in Yellowstone National Park. From there, with the help of a quart of bourbon, they managed to crash the Ford outside of Laurel, Montana. Hemingway suffered a bad break to his right arm and remained at St. Vincent's Hospital in Billings for two months. His hospital stay was the inspiration for the rollicking short story, "The Gambler, the Nun and the Radio." The crash was not the end of the "tin lizzy." After Hemingway returned to Key West, Chub Weaver drove the repaired Ford all the way from Montana to Key West, and then stayed on and fished the rest of the winter with the Hemingways. A year and half later the Ford made its return to the Yellowstone High Country. After a late bear hunt, Hemingway and longtime friend Charles Thompson had to wait for muddy roads to freeze before they could drive the old Ford out of a swamp. The two headed out in a blizzard and used a candle in a tin can on the dashboard to keep the windshield defrosted. That was the last the Yellowstone High Country saw of Hemingway's trusty Model A.

The Ranch

Lying about ten miles east of Cooke City, Montana, the L—T Ranch is one of several ranches in the area owned by wealthy families. Great care has been taken to preserve the ranches so they are very much the same as they were in Hemingway's day. The L—T in the 1930s was owned by two wealthy Chicago families: Copeland and Sidley. Lawrence Nordquist was commissioned to run it, earning a stake in the property by doing so. There was a main lodge and typical barns and corrals needed for running a cow-hay operation and dude ranch; irrigation water was provided by the Clark's Fork. There were a group of guest cabins in the trees. Cabin number one was the first cabin inhabited by Hemingway, Pauline, and Bumby. As the family grew and guests became more frequent, the family moved to the larger Sidley Cabin on a knoll by the river.

These ranches have a colorful history mainly due to their remoteness. The original owner of the L—T was shot by a ranch hand, and much of the stonework was done by a man who killed two people—one with an axe. After Hemingway's decade there, "Perry Mason" author Erle Stanley Gardner was a guest, as was artist Salvador Dali.

Ernest Hemingway and the future Mrs. Bunny Horne sit on the running board of Heming-way's 1928 Model A Ford Sport Coupe. Hemingway took the Ford on several trips to the Yellowstone High Country.

THE WYOMING ROOM, SHERIDAN COUNTY FULMER PUBLIC LIBRARY.

I

1928

In 1928, two years before his first visit to the Yellowstone High Country, Hemingway made an exploratory trip to Sheridan, Wyoming, and the nearby Bighorn Mountains. He had married his second wife, Pauline Pfeiffer, the year before. On June 28th Pauline gave birth to Patrick, their first child together. Hemingway had another son Jack or 'Bumby' (as he was called when he was young) from his previous marriage to Hadley Richardson.

At this point in his career, Hemingway had published *Three Short Stories and Ten Poems*, *The Torrents of Spring*, *In Our Time*, and *The Sun Also Rises*. He had also lived in Paris and socialized with F. Scott Fitzgerald, Gertrude Stein, and John Dos Passos. Before his time in Paris, Hemingway had volunteered in Italy as an ambulance driver during WWI, been the first American wounded on the Italian front, and then fallen in love with his nurse. Hemingway had used these experiences as subject matter for his latest work, which had been left unfinished and without a title.

Patrick's birth was difficult: eighteen hours of labor ending with a Caesarean section. Pauline's recovery was long and difficult and made worse by the suffocating summer heat of Kansas City. When Pauline was well enough to travel, the Hemingways took the train to Piggott, Arkansas, where her parents lived. A month after the birth, when Pauline and Patrick had gained enough strength, Ernest headed west. He had a novel to finish.[1]

Hemingway went back to Kansas City to pick up his Model A Ford and meet his friend Bill Horne.[2] Neither of the two men, who had met in Italy in the ambulance corps, had ever seen the Rocky Mountains. Feeling like explorers they crossed Kansas, a corner of Nebraska, and then followed the Platte River into Wyoming. Hemingway hoped some clean, cool mountain air, rising trout, and time away from the family and in-laws would allow him the time and space to finish his book.[3]

Hemingway had been asked to stay at a ranch in Jackson Hole, Wyoming, but Horne had been invited to a more remote spot outside of Sheridan, Wyoming.[4] Hemingway was taken by the beauty of the Bighorn Mountains there. This was his first summer away from Spain and its bullfight circuit in six years. Although he was looking for a new adventure, there was something comfortably familiar about his surroundings. In a letter to his longtime friend, painter Waldo Pierce, Hemingway wrote, "Looks like Spain, Bighorn Mts [ringers] for the Guadaramas only on a bigger scale. Same color, same shape."[5]

When Hemingway and his friend Bill Horne arrived at the Folly Ranch in Wyoming, sixteen young women were staying there. Hemingway (third from the right) soon moved on, but Horne (right) stayed at the ranch, courted a young woman named "Bunny," and eventually married her.
THE WYOMING ROOM, SHERIDAN COUNTY FULMER PUBLIC LIBRARY

Hemingway's Ford bounced over rocks and ruts up the steep, winding road to the ranch. As Hemingway steered around hairpin turns with steep drop-offs, Horne implored Hemingway to slow down and "look out." After enduring this for a while, Hemingway turned to his friend and said, "Do me favor, Horney. When you get out, just close the door."[6] After stopping at a spring to fill the car's radiator, they arrived at the Folly Ranch, 8,000 feet up on the eastern side of the Bighorns. They began their stay with fishing trips to the east fork of Big Goose Creek and Cross Creek, returning to the ranch for campfire dinners, singing around the piano, and storytelling.

There were sixteen girls staying at the Folly Ranch, and the creeks were full of trout. After writing four pages and catching twelve trout the first day, another four pages but only two trout on the second day, then thirty trout and no pages on the third day, Hemingway packed up and left. Horne had hit it off with a girl named Bunny, so Hemingway's abrupt departure allowed Bill the time to court the eventual Mrs. Bunny Horne.

Before going their separate ways, the two men scanned a map of the area, noticing a trout stream running towards the Montana-Wyoming border outside of Yellowstone's northeast corner. In a 1979 interview with the *Barrington Courier Review*, Horne remembered the first time Hemingway zeroed in on the Clark's Fork of the Yellowstone: "Horney," he said, "That's the place. Someday you and I'll go there and slaughter 'em!" Two years later the two friends would do just that.

Hemingway headed into town and booked a room at the Sheridan Inn, an old hotel once owned by Buffalo Bill Cody. He spent his days struggling to finish his new novel; his nights were spent drinking and playing poker at the Mint Bar downtown. In a letter he wrote, "I wish to God Pauline would come out and that I would get this book finished before she comes. Am lonely as a bastard, drank too much last night and feel like anything but work now."[7]

As eager as he was for the arrival of Pauline, the ending Hemingway had written for the novel was going to be a little difficult to explain. He had decided that the heroine Catherine, and the child she was carrying, both die during childbirth, an ending inspired by the traumatic delivery in Kansas City. In a

Hemingway finished his famous novel, A Farewell to Arms, *at the Sheridan Inn (shown here) in Sheridan, Wyoming, in 1928. It was Hemingway's first trip out west.*
THE WYOMING ROOM, SHERIDAN COUNTY FULMER PUBLIC LIBRARY.

July 27 letter sent to his friend and fellow journalist Guy Hickok from the Bighorn post office, Hemingway describes Patrick's birth: "Nearly killed Pauline… But everything alright finally and no one dead…." On August 23 in a letter to Waldo Pierce, Hemingway declared he had finished the novel.

While in Sheridan, Hemingway had befriended the Moncinis, a French family who lived on Val Vista Street a couple of blocks from the inn, on what was then the outskirts of town. The couple worked in the local coal mines and had two sons, August and Lucien. After baptizing young Patrick at the family chapel in Piggott, Pauline left him in the care of her parents and set off to meet her husband. She arrived at the Sheridan train station on August 18. Hemingway took her to meet his new friends. The Hemingways were able to speak French with their hosts while drinking their homemade wine. It was an amicable arrangement that Carlos Baker considered the source of the short story, "Wine of Wyoming." However, in a 1970 article in the *Casper Star-Tribune*, the Moncini's daughter, Lea Moncini Ahlstrom, disputed this assessment. She said another family, the Pichots, "who were our neighbors are identical to the 'Wine of Wyoming' couple."

The Hemingways spent the rest of their stay in the Bighorn Mountains at a ranch owned by former Wyoming Senator Willis Spear and his daughter Elsa, the Spear-O-Wigwam. Hemingway's visit was described in the *Casper Star-Tribune* in 1970: "The stone and log cabin in which the Hemingways lived sits at the edge of a clear amber stream. Inside, the furniture—the desk, chairs, beds—is of strong, rough logs, handmade more than 40 years before. Early in the morning, Hemingway could walk outside and look across the rushing stream, see cattle grazing on the hillside, moose and deer and elk feeding carelessly on the top."[8]

Ernest Hemingway with fly rod and fishing creel, circa 1928.
ERNEST HEMINGWAY COLLECTION. JOHN F. KENNEDY PRESIDENTIAL LIBRARY AND MUSEUM, BOSTON.

From here, Ernest and Pauline took an exploratory fishing trip up the Clark's Fork. After buying a new shotgun (Winchester 12 gauge pump),[9] they headed to Shell, Wyoming, to visit Owen Wister, author of *The Virginian*. Hemingway and Wister managed to shoot some some prairie dogs from the car, then stopped by the Crow Indian Reservation to

Pauline Pfeiffer Hemingway, shown here in 1928 in the Bighorn Mountains of Wyoming, wears her husband's Colt Woodsman semi-automatic pistol in a hip holster. Pauline was an accomplished bird hunter and angler.

ERNEST HEMINGWAY COLLECTION. JOHN F. KENNEDY PRESIDENTIAL LIBRARY AND MUSEUM, BOSTON.

shoot prairie chickens. The couple eventually pulled out of the Bighorns and into the town of Cody, through Yellowstone National Park, and out the park's South Entrance to Jackson Hole. They stopped to fish the Snake River, catching three large cutthroat trout, before turning east and back toward Arkansas.

As they returned from Hemingway's furthest venture west, the author had finished his novel, *A Farewell to Arms*, gathered the material for "Wine of Wyoming," and whet his appetite for the Rocky Mountains. This trip established a formula that would serve him well for the next eleven years. Whenever something needed finishing, he would head west for the summer and fall to a place where he could hunt, fish, and work. While he and Pauline would continue to catch trout, Hemingway would not have to settle for prairie dogs and chickens much longer: the big game of the Yellowstone High Country awaited.

Shortly after leaving Wyoming, Hemingway received word that his father had died. He headed to his childhood home of Oak Park, Michigan, and once there, found that his father had shot himself with an old, worn, Smith and Wesson .32 caliber revolver that had belonged to Anson Hemingway, Ernest's grandfather. While suicide in general would preoccupy Hemingway for the rest of his life, this particular event would haunt him for the next eleven years.

A couple of months after Hemingway's father's death, a box arrived at Ernest and Pauline's new home in Key West. Hemingway's mother, Grace, had mentioned sending some paintings that she wanted to sell, but Ernest wanted nothing to do with them. The box they came in sat for more than a month before Pauline insisted on opening it. Inside were the paintings, a now moldy chocolate cake, and the Smith and Wesson.[10] This gun would be with Hemingway when he returned to the mountains two years later.

Ernest Hemingway at the L—T Ranch in 1930.
PATRICK HEMINGWAY PAPERS, C0066, MANUSCRIPTS DIVISION, DEPARTMENT
OF RARE BOOKS AND SPECIAL COLLECTIONS, PRINCETON UNIVERSITY LIBRARY.

II

1930

As Ernest Hemingway drove west in 1930, though still only thirty, he had been to war, been married, divorced, and married again, had two sons, published two collections of short stories, and just finished his second novel. He'd lived most of the last ten years in France and Spain before returning home to be confronted by the death of his father and the birth of the Great Depression.

Hemingway's time in the Yellowstone High Country began on July 13, 1930, when he first crossed the Clark's Fork and settled onto the L—T Ranch ten miles outside of Cooke City, Montana. The ranch was owned by Olive and Lawrence Nordquist; the "L" and "T" stood for the first and last letters in the latter's name.

Hemingway arrived with his second wife, Pauline Pfeiffer, and his first son Jack, often called Bumby. Patrick, his second son and first with Pauline, stayed in Piggott, Arkansas, with Pauline's parents. Before arriving at the L—T, they had been directed to another ranch on Sunlight Creek owned by Simon Snyder.[1] People there, when they realized who their famous guest was, fawned and pandered to him to such a degree that the Hemingways piled into the car and ventured further upriver in search of a lower profile.

The main draw of this area was the Clark's Fork River and its spectacular trout fishing. Upon arrival, Hemingway entered the Clark's Fork Valley folklore by becoming the first person to drive a car all the way to the L—T Ranch. At that time the road was passable by automobiles only up to Crandall Creek; from there, people and supplies were taken in by horses. The Hemingway's Model A Ford, the same car which had made some famous runs from

Paris to Pamplona some years before[2], became high-centered on the deeply rutted horse-and-wagon road. Lawrence Nordquist came across them, pulled the Ford unstuck with his team of horses, and took them to his ranch. Nordquist, the ranch, and the valley in which it sat made an immediate impact on Hemingway, and he, in turn, made his own impression on the people at the ranch. In a later history of the area's ranches, Hemingway's arrival was noted as follows: "He was tall, slender, with dark hair, mustache and laughing black eyes. He was evidently pleased with the beauty of the country, and the primitive quality of the ranch. It was not long before Ernest and Pauline, in genuine friendliness, were very much a part of the group."[3]

Hemingway spent the first couple of weeks fishing the Clark's Fork and preparing his short story collection *In Our Time* for a second printing. Like all of his fiction, the stories in this collection were loosely autobiographical. They depict the coming of age of Nick Adams in northern Michigan. Because of the stories' roots in real life, the publisher had concerns about libel. On August 12 Hemingway headed into Cooke City with a letter to Max Perkins, his friend and editor. "Dear Max, have gone over I.O.T. also the 'Up in Michigan.' I've re-written it to keep it from being libelous but to do so takes all the character away...." Hemingway would find himself in this position throughout his career: consistently deciding to keep things brutally honest regardless of whom he offended. The work on *In Our Time* seems to have been a distraction during this period, with Hemingway eager to put it behind him in favor of his new project. Since arriving in the valley, he had worked six days a week writing 40,000 words and showing no signs of slowing down. He wrote to Perkins, "Have six more cases of beer good for six more chapters—if I put in an expense account for this new bullfight book it would be something for the accounting department to study."[4] The bullfighting book would become *Death in the Afternoon.*

Pauline fished with her husband and kept an eye on Jack, who at seven was fascinated with the art of fly fishing. His father, however, had rules: Bumby could tag along if they were fishing close to the ranch but only if he didn't spook the trout.[5]

Hemingway spent his time working on his bullfighting book and getting to

Pauline Pfiffer, Hemingway's wife, often fly fished with him. Here, wearing waders, she sits beside the Clark's Fork.
Ernest Hemingway Collection. John F. Kennedy Presidential Library and Museum, Boston.

Jack (Bumby) Hemingway at the ranch in 1930. He loved to ride horses.
Patrick Hemingway Papers, C0066, Manuscripts Division, Department of Rare Books and Special Collections, Princeton University Library.

know the ranch hands: gleaning information, drinking, and developing friendships with men such as Floyd Allington, Smokey Royce, and Huck Mees. Allington, an expert fisherman (and bootlegger), talked fishing with Hemingway the whole summer. The writer told the guide that he considered the Clark's Fork of the Yellowstone to be the best trout fishing in the world. He also developed friendships with Ivan Wallace, John Staebe, and Leland Stanford Weaver, known as "Chub." Wallace and Hemingway hit it off right away with Wallace knowing just the right buttons to push, as shown by this conversation between them as recorded in the Carlos Baker biography of Hemingway:

Ivan: "How about a little fishing this morning?"

Ernest: "Can't do it, got to work."

A half hour later....

Ernest: "Ivan, you've ruined the working day for me. Let's go fishing."[6]

Wallace worked at the L—T from 1930 to 1932. In 1970 he told reporter Addison Bragg of the *Billings Gazette* that, "Hemingway could be lured away from his writing by nothing more complicated than a friendly drink and talk....I guess I probably knew him when he was happiest...when times were good and happy...." In the same article, Laura Weaver recalled, "They were quite a threesome, Ernest Hemingway, Chub, who had a nose for game and was an excellent camp cook, and Ivan, a very good fisherman and fishing guide."[7] Of all the men at the ranch, Hemingway was closest to Chub Weaver, and the two would remain friends for the rest of their lives.

Between rainstorms, Hemingway fished the Clark's Fork with moderate success until his buddy Bill Horne arrived with his new wife Bunny. Ernest and Bill hit the river and landed 49 good rainbows using fishing flies named "McGinty's" and "Grey Palmers." Hemingway had not always been a fly fisherman, as his eldest son points out in his foreword to *Hemingway on Fishing*: "'Big Two Hearted River' more than made that point, as did 'The Last Good Country' and the trout fishing on the Irati in *The Sun Also Rises*." In the "The Last Good Country," Nick Adams rolls over a log and finds a couple of worms, hooks them, and catches a brook trout from under the bank. In *The Sun Also Rises,* Jake Barnes fishes Spain's Irati River with his friend Bill and they head different directions on the river. Jake opts for the bait can and Bill opts for the fly box. In "Big Two-Hearted River: Part II" Nick Adams uses a fly rod but with live grasshoppers; he wades into the river and drops a hooked grasshopper into the water, letting it drift until taken, no flies and no casting. According to his eldest son, by the time Hemingway made it to the Yellowstone High Country he was a fly fisherman, "I remember that when we went to L Bar T Ranch near Cook City...there was a wide

Two of Hemingway's best friends at the L—T Ranch were ranch hands Ivan Wallace (left)
"a very good fisherman and fishing guide" and Chub Weaver (right) "who had a nose for
game and was an excellent camp cook."
Ernest Hemingway Collection. John F. Kennedy Presidential Library and Museum,
Boston.

selection of Hardy [fly fishing] tackle…"[8] Later, when a Hardy tackle box
containing all of Hemingway's fly fishing gear was lost on a train to Sun
Valley, the loss effectively ended his love affair with the fly.

In his book *The Misadventures of a Fly Fisherman,* Jack Hemingway gives us
a little more insight into his father's fishing tackle and strategy: "Papa was a
pretty straight-forward wet fly fisherman. He used Hardy tackle and his leaders
were already tied up with three flies. His favorites were a McGinty for the top,
a cock-y-bondhu for the middle, and a woodcock green for the tail fly. He
sometimes fished with single-eyed flies and added a dropper. At the ranch, for
these, he preferred a Hardy's worm fly and the shrimp fly. Ninety percent of

Virtually all of Hemingway's fly fishing was in the Yellowstone High Country. Here he poses with fresh caught trout.
ERNEST HEMINGWAY COLLECTION. JOHN F. KENNEDY PRESIDENTIAL LIBRARY AND MUSEUM, BOSTON.

the time, Papa was an across and downstream caster whose team of flies swam or skittered across the current so that a fish taking one pretty much hooked itself."[9] Hemingway explained the effectiveness of that three-fly rig in *Green Hills of Africa*: "Rigged up my rod and made a cast and it was dark and there was a nighthawk swooping around and it was cold as a bastard and then I was fast to three fish the second the flies hit the water."

As August progressed, heavy rainfall muddied the river and on August 21 the Hornes left. The next morning Smokey Royce, Chub Weaver, Ivan Wallace, and Ernest Hemingway set out to check on a bear bait up the north fork of Crandall Creek. Ralph Glidden tells the story in his *History of the Cooke City Area*:

> Hemingway was riding a skittish mare named Goofy when she bolted into the trees. A sharp branch sliced Hemingway's chin, and neither him or Ivan were able to stop the bleeding. Borrowing a car from the [Forest] Ranger at Crandall Creek they sped to the nearest doctor in Cody [Wyoming]. The doctor wanted to put the writer to sleep but all Hemingway wanted was some whiskey. Finally they got a bottle of Old Oscar Pepper and Hemingway's work was completed.[10]

Hemingway and Wallace had arrived in Cody at midnight and the only doctor they could find was a converted veterinarian named Dr. Trueblood. The bootleg whiskey the doctor had on hand was apparently unacceptable, so at Hemingway's urging, the good doctor wrote and filled a prescription for Old Oscar Pepper, a Kentucky bourbon that during Prohibition was available only for "medicinal purposes." The Crandall Ranger had sent his daughter with the two men to look after the car. As she drove the two men back from Cody, she had to stop regularly to open cattle gates and pass through. At each of these stops Hemingway and Wallace would take another pull from the bottle. At the ranch they slept it off for the first part of the next day, then headed back up to the dead horse that Wallace had left for bear bait.

After an experience Hemingway couldn't have written or dreamed up (with Ivan, Smokey, and Chub, riding a horse named Goofy, patched up by a veterinarian-turned-doctor named Trueblood, and using a little help from Oscar Pepper), Hemingway shot his first bear. It was a large, brown-colored black bear. The last of the whiskey was used to get through the skinning of the bear, which had picked up most of the maggots from the rotting horse. The next day, upon returning to the L—T, Hemingway approached Lawrence Nordquist about buying Goofy. Nordquist tried to discourage him, saying there were far better saddle horses in his stable he could buy. Hemingway growled through his newly stitched up face, "I don't want to ride him, I want to shoot him for bear bait."[11] Hemingway had to return to Cody to have his chin re-stitched. Before leaving, he went into the corral and ripped long strands of hair from Goofy for the doctor to use for the stitching thread.[12]

By the time this episode ended, the river had cleared and the fish were rising. After a couple of weeks fishing and generally enjoying late summer in the mountains, Pauline and Jack left the ranch on September 14 as the men prepared for the opening day of hunting season. Hemingway's excitement about the upcoming season is conveyed in a September 10 letter to Henry (Mike) Strater: "Take the train to Gardiner, MT. Stage will bring you to Cooke City - I'll meet you there with horses… License 60 bucks gives you 1 elk, 1 deer, 1 bear, game birds and trout. 15 bucks extra for mountain sheep."[13] The letter provides a glimpse into what the north side of Yellowstone was like at the time; there hasn't been a train to Gardiner or stage coaches through Yellowstone for a long time, and the horse trail between the ranch and Cooke City became part of US Highway 212.

That fall the hunting would not disappoint. First, Hemingway took a bighorn sheep. After a two-day ride he headed up Pilot Creek, this time on a horse he loved. Old Bess was a black mare with a white stripe on her face. He was able to take her on the sheep trails, rock slides, and boulder fields flanking Pilot and Index peaks and shoot a big ram with a heavy curl. This was the only time Hemingway shot a bighorn sheep and he shot it under the great peaks. In an article for *Vogue* magazine, Hemingway wrote: "The old ram was purple-grey, his rump was white, and when he raised his head you saw the great heavy curl of his horns. It was the white of his rump that had betrayed him to you in the green of the junipers when you had lain in the lee of a rock, out of the wind, three miles away, looking carefully at every yard of the high country through a pair of good Zeiss glasses."[14] Hemingway would return to these same slopes two years later with his friend Charles Thompson, this time hunting for nine days with no luck, enduring what he called the "Damndest ledge work you ever saw."[15]

Next there was his first bull elk. Hemingway and Wallace were bugling for

Hemingway instructed a friend who was coming to the ranch: "Take the train to Gardiner, MT. Stage will bring you to Cooke City – I'll meet you there with horses." This photo shows the horse trail leading to Cooke City, Montana, circa 1930.
PHOTO PROVIDED BY THE AUTHOR.

Hemingway glasses for bighorn sheep. He later wrote: "It was the white of his rump that had betrayed him to you in the green of the junipers when you had lain in the lee of a rock, out of the wind, three miles away, looking carefully at every yard of the high country through a pair of good Zeiss glasses."
PHOTO COURTESY OF DINK BRUCE.

The wilderness outpost of Cooke City, Montana, in 1930, the year of Hemingway's arrival.
PHOTO PROVIDED BY THE AUTHOR.

Hemingway looks for bighorn sheep while his favorite horse, Old Bess, stands with loose reins.
PHOTO COURTESY OF DINK BRUCE.

Hemingway poses with with the only bighorn sheep he ever shot, a full-curl ram.
PHOTO COURTESY OF DINK BRUCE.

Hemingway was at home among the mountain men and cowboys of the Yellowstone High Country.
Photo courtesy of Dink Bruce.

elk (imitating the call of a bull elk) in some thick timber when they heard a reply from an adjacent draw. They spotted the elk in trees beside a meadow and crawled so close that through binoculars "they could see his chest muscles swell as he lifted his head" to reveal a trophy 6 x 6 rack.[16] Heart racing, Hemingway waited for the bull to step into the meadow, and as it dropped its head to feed, he squeezed the trigger of his Springfield rifle, taking the elk with a single shot.

While Henry Strater didn't visit the ranch that fall, Hemingway's friend and fellow author John Dos Passos sent word that he was coming. Before he arrived, Hemingway and Wallace took another trip up Crandall Creek. On this trip, Hemingway met John Staebe and his first grizzly bear. Staebe, who would later appear in *Green Hills of Africa* as "John Staib," was a German WWI veteran who had homesteaded the Ghost Creek Ranch near Crandall.[17] Although deaf, he was a mountain man of the highest order and was well respected by all of the hands at the L—T. The grizzly bear would make an even deeper impression on Hemingway as he would remember it nine years later: "You heard a crash of timber and thought it was a cow elk bolting, and then there they were, in the broken shadow, running with an easy, lurching smoothness, the afternoon sun making their coats a soft bristling silver."[18]

On October 21, Dos Passos arrived in Billings and headed to the ranch. He had a license for elk, but he was nearsighted and had little knowledge of hunting and firearms. He later remarked that Hemingway "had the ranch hands under his thumb."[19] Dos Passos, the outsider in the group, seems to have misread the reciprocal relationship forming between Hemingway and the men at the ranch. While he may well have had them under his spell, he was most certainly under theirs. For ten days they travelled the high country: Timber Creek, Crandall Creek, and the Crazy Lakes. Hemingway and the ranch hands hunted while Dos Passos enjoyed the scenery.

On Halloween night the two writers, along with Floyd Allington, piled into Hemingway's Ford with warm clothes, blankets, and a quart of bourbon. Allington's fishing prowess had convinced Hemingway to drag him south to ply his skills in the waters off Key West. Allington was excited enough at the idea that he was willing to ride in the rumble seat, wrapped in blankets. The unlikely trio drove through Cooke City and the northern part of Yellowstone, camping for the night at Mammoth Hot Springs "within earshot of the retching gurgle of a warm geyser."[20] The following morning they headed out of the park, through Paradise Valley and Livingston, and on toward Billings. Just after dusk outside of Laurel, they drove into a ditch. Since "loose gravel," "the lights of an oncoming car," and "a car backing out of a driveway" were all given as reasons for the crash, it is easy to assume that the bourbon might have had something to do with it.

Hemingway broke his arm and Allington dislocated a shoulder, but Dos Passos escaped unscathed. A passing motorist picked them up and drove them to St. Vincent's Hospital in Billings. Hemingway rode in the back seat with his arm pinned between his knees. Upon checking in, Hemingway was asked his occupation and he replied "writer." The receptionist, taking in his appearance, wrote on the form "rider."[21] The break was serious, an oblique spiral fracture above the elbow, nearly compound, and Hemingway spent the next seven weeks at St. Vincent's. Three years later a graphic description of the wound would appear in *Green Hills of Africa*: "...one time in a hospital with my right arm broken off short between the elbow and the shoulder, the back of the hand having hung down against my back, the points of the bone having cut up the flesh of the biceps until it finally rotted, swelled, burst, and sloughed off in pus."

While hunting in East Africa, Hemingway would see his injury as crucial to his development as a hunter. In *Green Hills of Africa*, Hemingway wrote: "Alone with the pain in the night in the fifth week of not sleeping I thought suddenly how a bull elk must feel if you break a shoulder and he gets away and in that night I lay and felt it all, the whole thing as it would happen from the shock of the bullet to the end of the business and, being a little out of my head, thought perhaps what I was going through was a punishment for all hunters....Since I still loved to hunt I resolved that I would only shoot as long I could kill cleanly and as soon as I lost that ability I would stop."[22] Hemingway had just experienced the best hunting of his life. Although he had shot deer and squirrels as a youth, his experiences in the Yellowstone High Country were on a different level.

In the hospital he was treated by Sister Florence Cloonan, entertained by his small transistor radio, and accompanied in his misery by a Mexican gambler who had been shot twice in the gut over a card game. He was fond of Sister Florence and must have had a sense of déjà vu given his relationship with Agnes Von Kurosky during his lengthy hospital stay in Italy during WWI, fictionalized in *A Farewell to Arms*. The gambler, with his stoic acceptance of his fate, compares well with other characters in Hemingway's short fiction, such as Ole Anderson in "The Killers" who, like the Mexican, "follows his own stoical code and refuses to denounce his assailants."[23] He is certainly kin to Blindie in "A Man of the World," who also refuses to condemn the man who wronged him. In fact, wounding and injury, and how men deal with them physically and psychologically, is a major theme throughout Hemingway's work: Frederick Henry's injury is central to *A Farewell to Arms*; Harry Morgan of *To Have and Have Not* loses an arm; In *For Whom the Bell Tolls,* Robert Jordan breaks a leg, and so on. As Hemingway lay in St. Vincent's, he was dealing with the second serious injury of his first trip to the Yellowstone High Country and the physical and emotional demands that came with them. This episode and its details would work its way into *Green Hills of Africa, For Whom the Bell Tolls*, and was perhaps the blueprint for the irrational, pain- and alcohol-influenced behavior of Harry, the narrator of Hemingway's short story masterpiece, "The Snows of Kilimanjaro."

Hemingway's stay at St. Vincent's was covered by Carlos Baker in his biography and in a Montana Public Broadcasting television documentary entitled *Paradise and Purgatory: Hemingway at the L—T and St. Vincent's Hospital.* However, the most entertaining account of the hospital stay is from Hemingway himself.

The riotous short story "The Gambler, the Nun and the Radio" is, according to the author, an absolutely true account of his long stay in Billings. Towards the end of his stay, as his arm healed, Hemingway was able to leave the hospital for short periods of time. He visited the home of his doctor, a renowned orthopedic surgeon named Dr. Allard. The doctor "who liked Hemingway personally, found his writing distasteful and often took him to task for the

Hemingway poses in St. Vincent's Hospital in Billings, Montana, recovering from a badly broken arm suffered in a car crash on his way out of the Yellowstone High Country in 1930.
PHOTO PROVIDED BY THE AUTHOR.

language he employed--so much so that Allard's son Joe remembered that he and his brother and sister were afraid at times that Hemingway, who appeared to the children to be a 'bear of a man,' would beat up their father."[24]

After leaving the hospital, Hemingway and Pauline traveled to her family home in Piggott, Arkansas, for Christmas. One day while out walking, still limping and unshaven, Hemingway was labelled a tramp by a large group of school children who chased him through the streets and hurled snowballs at him. He had to take shelter in a stranger's house,[25] and it was here he met Otto (Toby) Bruce, who would become Hemingway's driver, handyman, and friend for the next thirty years. Bruce would help shuttle the Hemingway family to and from the ranch for the rest of the decade and even built the wall that still surrounds the Hemingway home in Key West.[26] The episode quickly turned Hemingway's dislike for Piggott into hatred, and the Hemingways soon headed back to Key West.

The accident and recuperation may have soured the memory of that first year in the Yellowstone High Country, but by the new year the experience had allowed him to finish his page proofs for the reissue of *In Our Time,* craft *Death in the Afternoon* almost in its entirety, and accrue the experience that would later become "The Gambler, the Nun and the Radio." Along with the best trout fishing of his life, he had also shot his first bear, elk, and sheep, saw his first grizzly bear, and accumulated a few new scars and several new friends. Although Floyd Allington missed the chance to accompany Hemingway to Key West because of the car wreck, Chub Weaver seized the opportunity and delivered the repaired Ford to Hemingway and stayed the rest of the winter for the fishing. Olive and Lawrence Nordquist flew to Key West and by Valentine's Day in 1931, just over a month and a half since the writer had left Montana, the Hemingways, the Nordquists, and Chub Weaver were fishing together again, 3,000 miles from the L—T. It was about this time that Hemingway found out that Pauline was pregnant with Gregory, his third son and second with Pauline. The baby was due in November, which meant the couple would not be able to return to the ranch that year.

After traveling to Spain to gather pictures for the finalizing of *Death in the*

Afternoon, the Hemingways returned to the states for Pauline to give birth. Hemingway had been planning a trip to Africa the next year with his friends Charles Thompson, Henry Strater, and Archie MacLeish. The research had been done and arrangements had been made. In April 1932 however, McCleish bowed out, and by June, Hemingway had done the same. He suggested his eyesight and the political and social turmoil in America as his excuses, while in reality, Pauline's uncle was reluctant to fund the trip that summer. This, coupled with his enthusiasm for a return to the L—T Ranch and the months of fishing and hunting it would provide, convinced Hemingway to postpone his first African safari in favor of a return to the Yellowstone High Country. "One more motivating factor was that he was seething with 'damned good stories' that he wanted to tell."[27]

Hemingway was invigorated by his life in the high mountains. Here he poses at one of the remote Crazy Lakes on a backcountry fishing trip.

III

1932

On July 12, 1932, the Hemingways crossed the Clark's Fork and settled back into cabin number one at the L—T Ranch. Hemingway was obviously happy to be back. Prohibition, the approaching civil war in Spain, the Great Depression, and the upcoming U.S. presidential election all seemed a world away. Hemingway spent his first couple of days reacquainting himself with the sights, sounds, and smells of the ranch and the Clark's Fork Valley, including the aroma of sage penetrated by the smell of trout, bacon, and onions wafting from the ranch kitchen. Rising early each morning, he watched sunlight illuminate Pilot and Index peaks and ease down the slopes that he had hunted on two years before.

After the Hemingway's first visit to the ranch in 1930, they had received a steady stream of visitors to their home in Key West. The Nordquists and Chub Weaver visited in the spring of 1931, and the Sidleys, part owners of the L—T, visited in the summer of that same year. During their visit, while Hemingway and Mr. Sidley were offshore fishing, Pauline and Mrs. Sidley went swimming at the Bayview Park pool. While it is unclear what exactly happened, Mrs. Sidley almost drowned in the pool and was thought to be dead when she was pulled ashore by Pauline. She was resuscitated and taken to recover at the Hemingway home.[1] From that moment forward the Hemingway family was granted access to the Sidley Cabin whenever they visited the ranch. This cabin was bigger and perched right above the river. Olive Nordquist remembered seeing Hemingway "emerge(s) from the door, wiping his glasses, squinting at

Pilot (left) and Index peaks as seen from cabin number one at the L—T Ranch. Heming-way stayed in cabin number one during his first year at the ranch.
ERNEST HEMINGWAY COLLECTION. JOHN F. KENNEDY PRESIDENTIAL LIBRARY AND MUSEUM, BOSTON.

the intense blue of the cloudless sky, gazing at Index…inflating his lungs with the clean air, and padding softly back in his moccasins for another hour at the desk."[2] While he had no novel in progress this summer, Hemingway did have time to finish the short story "The Light of the World."[3] He would write in longhand and Pauline would type his words between trips to fish, pick wild berries, or shoot game birds. After pulling Mrs. Sidley from the pool in Key West and holding her own on fishing trips and bird hunts, Pauline, with her fly rod, her 28 gauge shotgun, and her cocktail recipes, had gained the respect of everyone at the L—T.

At the ranch Hemingway renewed his friendships with Ivan Wallace and

Pauline Hemingway stands with Chub Weaver on a sheep hunting trip after losing her Stetson hat when strong winds on a steep ridge blew it off.
PATRICK HEMINGWAY PAPERS, C0066, MANUSCRIPTS DIVISION, DEPARTMENT OF RARE BOOKS AND SPECIAL COLLECTIONS, PRINCETON UNIVERSITY LIBRARY.

Chub Weaver. Prohibition was still the law of the land, but Red Lodge moonshine was readily available. The Allington brothers, among others, would run shipments of Red Lodge's finest products over the 10,947-foot Beartooth Pass. According to Laura Weaver, a typical order—if guests were expected—would be two barrels of wine and a case of whiskey, some of which was always waiting next to a bucket of ice in Hemingway's cabin at the end of each day.[4] While periodically working on short stories, he had no major works in progress. With hunting season still two months away, Hemingway had time to relax and properly settle into life at the ranch. In an interview with Denis Brian, Olive Nordquist recalled the summer of 1932 with her famous guests:

He was always being kind and considerate of people and took great care with his son Bumby. Somebody had to always be with the boy. I think he feared kidnapping. This was the time of the Lindberg baby kidnapping. The Hemingways were staying at our ranch in Wyoming. We were sitting in the lodge and it was Bumby's bedtime. It was dark and the boy was only 5 or 6 years old. We knew he was afraid to walk across the ranch alone but no one knew what to say without embarrassing him. All of a sudden Ernest jumped up! "Damn" he said "I forgot something at the cabin. I'll have to walk back with you Bumby."[5]

While Gregory Hemingway was too young to remember this incident, it didn't surprise him: "He was always considerate of our fears of the dark, he said he'd been so afraid of the dark after his injury in Italy he had to sleep with the light on for six months."[6] Gregory would later tell Joan Haines of the Associated Press: "Some of my happiest memories are of the days we spent at a Cooke City ranch with my father."[7]

The Hemingways' activities in the Yellowstone High Country were naturally divided between summer and fall. Summer was spent fishing the Clark's Fork and its contributing creeks and enjoying ranch life with Pauline and the boys. There were trips on horseback, on foot, and in the Ford to Cooke City and Cody, and once even to Powell, Wyoming, so Pauline could attend First Friday Mass. In an interview for Montana PBS, Patrick Hemingway remembered his parents during this time: "My dad and my mother were both fly fisherman, in fact they would fish together—they'd wet fly fish, one on one side of the river and one on the other side. Fishing was very much an ingredient in that marriage."[8]

In September, the Hemingways entertained their friends Gerald and Sara Murphy. They had known the Murphys since their time in Paris. They were very much a high society couple and had helped finance some of the "lost generation" during the lean years in Paris. While the food at the ranch did not impress the Murphys, the beauty of the place did. Hemingway took the family up to the

Hemingway, in riding chaps, poses with Gerald and Sara Murphy in 1932. The Murphys, who were friends with the Hemingways in Paris, visited them at the L—T Ranch.
PATRICK HEMINGWAY PAPERS, C0066, MANUSCRIPTS DIVISION, DEPARTMENT OF RARE BOOKS AND SPECIAL COLLECTIONS, PRINCETON UNIVERSITY LIBRARY.

Crazy Lakes to camp and fish and then took Gerald up Pilot Creek. In *Sara & Gerald: Villa America and After,* a 1982 memoir about her parents, Honoria Murphy Donnelly gave a detailed description of her three weeks at the ranch as well as a particularly specific account of the camping trip to the Crazy Lakes.

In her book, Honoria tells charming stories about combing and braiding her favorite horse's hair (to the amusement of the ranch hands) and of her parents distaste for the ranch food, especially the dessert of canned fruit cocktail served over iceberg lettuce with a dollop of mayonnaise and a cherry. She describes the ride up to the lakes and the ability of the horses to squeeze between trees, their arrival at the lake, the unpacking of the horses, the pitching of tents, and the potatoes and steaks sizzling on the fire.

*Mugging for the camera, wranglers on the Heming-
way-Murphy backcountry fishing trip exaggerate their
struggle to pack a horse.*
PATRICK HEMINGWAY PAPERS, C0066, MANUSCRIPTS DIVI-
SION, DEPARTMENT OF RARE BOOKS AND SPECIAL COLLEC-
TIONS, PRINCETON UNIVERSITY LIBRARY.

*The Hemingways and Murphys arrive at one of the
Crazy Lakes on their fishing trip. They camped by the
lakeshore.*
PATRICK HEMINGWAY PAPERS, C0066, MANUSCRIPTS DIVI-
SION, DEPARTMENT OF RARE BOOKS AND SPECIAL COLLEC-
TIONS, PRINCETON UNIVERSITY LIBRARY.

Hemingway poses with Honoria Murphy, the fourteen-year-old daughter of close friends Gerald and Sara Murphy. Hemingway taught Honoria how to fish, an experience she fondly recounted years later in her memoir.
PATRICK HEMINGWAY PAPERS, C0066, MANUSCRIPTS DIVISION, DE-PARTMENT OF RARE BOOKS AND SPECIAL COLLECTIONS, PRINCETON UNIVERSITY LIBRARY.

The next morning the group split into two boats. Pauline, Gerald, Sarah, and their son Baoth took the larger boat while Hemingway and Honoria took the other. These two unlikely fishing buddies crossed the lake, killed the motor, and Hemingway rowed gently while Honoria trolled a lure behind the boat until she felt a tug. Upon landing the fish, Hemingway unhooked it and announced that he would now show the girl how to clean a trout. After Honoria squealed and protested, he calmed her down and proceeded with what she later described as an "enchanting explanation of the design and function of the fish."

Honoria quoted Hemingway as saying: "First of all they have a rough skin protection, called scales, and we are going to have to scrape them off. Now, notice how the fish is shaped – it is narrow at the tail so it can glide through the water. Fish are clean, because they only eat things that live in the water. Can you see how the inside of the gills look like pink coral? And can you appreciate its beauty? Look at the silver line of its underbelly and the fine feathery lines of its fins. Don't they look like lace?"

After scaling the fish, Hemingway gave his knife to Honoria and guided her through the gutting and cleaning of it. As she became squeamish, he reiterated his point about the cleanliness of trout because of their habitat and diet. Then he explained the arrangement of their inner organs. He said, "See here, daughter, the lungs look like deep pink sponges, don't they? They're right inside the gill slits, where they are protected. The fish breathes by opening and closing those gill slits, letting the water in and out, just as we breathe air."[9] They caught a few more trout as did the crew in the other boat and they all headed back to camp. The grown-ups drank whiskey and cooked the fish over an open fire. Honoria wrote that she "had never tasted fish like that—they were sweet like nectar."[10] While much has changed since 1932, the trout in the Beartooth Mountains are still the best tasting freshwater fish in the world.

Honoria Murphy Donnelly's memories show us different side of Hemingway. As harsh as he could be to friends, critics, and fellow writers, he seemed to have a way with children, both his own and those of friends. He taught his sons to ride horses, fish, and shoot. He taught the Murphy's daughter how to catch and clean fish. The Murphys had three children: Baoth, Patrick, and Honoria.

In her memoir, Honoria Murphy wrote that she had "never tasted fish" like the trout she and Hemingway caught in a high-country lake and then cooked over a campfire. She wrote, "they were sweet like nectar."

PATRICK HEMINGWAY PAPERS, C0066, MANUSCRIPTS DIVISION, DEPARTMENT OF RARE BOOKS AND SPECIAL COLLECTIONS, PRINCETON UNIVERSITY LIBRARY.

Hemingway and Baoth Murphy with trout caught at one of the Crazy Lakes in 1932.

PATRICK HEMINGWAY PAPERS, C0066, MANUSCRIPTS DIVISION, DEPARTMENT OF RARE BOOKS AND SPECIAL COLLECTIONS, PRINCETON UNIVERSITY LIBRARY.

Hemingway holds up two large trout caught at a mountain lake. In her memoir, Honoria Murphy wrote, "Hemingway, who had to catch more rainbows than anybody, made big campfires at night and sat around with the kids in a goofy Tyrolean hat, roasting marshmallows and telling scary stories."
PATRICK HEMINGWAY PAPERS, C0066, MANUSCRIPTS DIVISION, DEPARTMENT OF RARE BOOKS AND SPECIAL COLLECTIONS, PRINCETON UNIVERSITY LIBRARY.

Within three years of this trip the two boys would be dead, Patrick from tuberculosis and Baoth from spinal meningitis. After describing the ranch trip in her memoir, Honoria includes a long letter written by Hemingway to her ailing brother Patrick in 1935. She also recalls that even as many friends were reluctant to visit her house because of Patrick's contagiousness, "Ernest came twice to our winter house in town shortly before Patrick died." Twenty-six years later Hemingway would write the last letter of his life to a nine-year-old boy hospitalized with heart disease. Indeed, Honoria Donnelly would remember, "Of all her parents famous friends and unfamous ones as well, it was Hemingway who paid closest attention to her and her brothers, who seemed to care for and understand each one of them as if they were his own.…Hemingway who had to catch more rainbows than anybody, made big campfires at night and sat around with the kids in a goofy Tyrolean hat, roasting marshmallows, telling scary stories."[11]

The fall was spent hunting. Long-time friend and hunting companion Charles Thompson arrived at the ranch for the season. Thompson was one of Hemingway's closest friends. He was from Key West and was instrumental in Hemingway's mastery of saltwater fishing and provided inspiration for the Harry Morgan character in *To Have and Have Not*. His brother Norberg served as mayor of Key West and was honored by a memorial sculpture and a statue at Lands End Marina at the south end of the island. A year after visiting Hemingway at the L—T, Thompson joined him in Africa.

Soon after Thompson's arrival, Hemingway, Pauline, Thompson, Ivan Wallace, and Chub Weaver headed up Pilot Creek to hunt bighorn sheep where two years earlier Hemingway had shot the first and only bighorn of his life. During this difficult hunt, Pauline had her Stetson hat blown off her head while high on a ridge, and Thompson, who had just arrived from sea level, struggled with the harsh terrain and altitude. They did find some sheep but could not get close enough to shoot as Hemingway explained in an October 14 letter sent from the ranch: "We took a beating on sheep. I stalked 8 rams, spooked them all. Charles stalked 11. That sheep hunting is what gave Charles hell. Damndest ledge work you ever saw. I had to take my shoes off on one mountain for about two miles on a rock slide. Fell 9 times. Never got a shot at a ram—if you're a good climber you could have got a ram. I'm not a good climber."[12]

Because the six-day sheep hunt was unsuccessful, the hunting party decided to head down country. Pauline traveled back to Key West while the men continued hunting. Their next trip was a thirty-five mile ride to Timber Creek for bear and elk. It was Thompson who shot the first elk of the season, a large bull. Hemingway then shot one and they shot one together. Ivan Wallace and Chub Weaver were both engaged to be married later that year and the group had four licenses between them, allowing Hemingway and Thompson to shoot

Hemingway looks at home in front of a wall tent at the Pilot Creek hunting camp in 1932. PATRICK HEMINGWAY PAPERS, C0066, MANUSCRIPTS DIVISION, DEPARTMENT OF RARE BOOKS AND SPECIAL COLLECTIONS, PRINCETON UNIVERSITY LIBRARY.

Hemingway traverses a steep slope while hunting for bighorn sheep. He later wrote to a friend, "I had to take my shoes off on one mountain for about two miles on a rock slide. Fell 9 times." PATRICK HEMINGWAY PAPERS, C0066, MANUSCRIPTS DIVISION, DEPARTMENT OF RARE BOOKS AND SPECIAL COLLECTIONS, PRINCETON UNIVERSITY LIBRARY.

Pauline Hemingway by one of the tents at the Pilot Creek Camp. PATRICK HEMINGWAY PAPERS, C0066, MANUSCRIPTS DIVISION, DEPARTMENT OF RARE BOOKS AND SPECIAL COLLECTIONS, PRINCETON UNIVERSITY LIBRARY.

Hemingway poses with a big bull elk taken on the hunting trip with Charles Thompson, a good friend and hunting partner from Key West, Florida. PATRICK HEMINGWAY PAPERS, C0066, MANUSCRIPTS DIVISION, DEPARTMENT OF RARE BOOKS AND SPECIAL COLLECTIONS, PRINCETON UNIVERSITY LIBRARY.

freely. By the end of the season they had "Killed enough meat for two guides to get married on—"[13]

One night, after a celebratory evening of elk steaks, moonshine, and story-telling around the campfire, Hemingway confided his feelings on suicide to Chub Weaver, saying "he would never hesitate to kill himself if the conditions were bad enough."[14] Although some of Hemingway's happiest days were at the Wyoming ranch, suicide was a theme that ran throughout his time there. His father had killed himself shortly before his first trip out west and even though he considered his father's suicide cowardly, he didn't consider all suicide that way, often hinting that it might be his own fate. The fact that he had this discussion with Chub Weaver indicated that Weaver was entering into Hemingway's innermost circle of friends.

As for his writing that summer, Hemingway was mostly editing and answering his critics. In July, he sent his final proofs for *Death in the Afternoon* to Max Perkins: "Hope you get these proofs and letter pretty fast am sending them in to Gardner—64 miles—to get them out today. ...You haven't even asked me what title goes on the front piece."[15] At the end of the same letter is evidence of the beginning of the deterioration of the relationship between Hemingway and F. Scott Fitzgerald: "Poor old Scott. He should have swapped Zelda when she was still at her craziest but still saleable back 5 or 6 years ago before she was diagnosed as nutty. He is the great tragedy of talent in our bloody generation. Well here comes the truck—must stop. So long Max—good luck."[16] The final line of this letter implies an image of Hemingway sitting on the stoop of the Cooke City General Store with the final version of *Death in the Afternoon* (published the following September) bundled under his arm and scribbling about the demise of F. Scott Fitzgerald while waiting for the mail truck to arrive from Gardiner. The remoteness of the ranch gave Hemingway the freedom and adventure he needed while his connection to the outpost town of Cooke City allowed him to keep up with his work and the goings on of the world outside.

In his next letter to Perkins on August 9, also from Cooke City, Hemingway gave his final go ahead for the publication of *Death in the Afternoon*, and while he must have been excited to finish the manuscript, his real excitement seemed to be toward the life he was living and discovering in the Yellowstone High Country: "We have been down sage grouse shooting for five days—finest shooting ever in my life—went down last Wednesday—shot limit everyday—Never shot better—would have given anything for you to be there—Just got back today and found final proofs—hit rock and broke bottom of engine - oil pan or crank case—coasted 4 miles back to Cooke."[17] From here, he goes on to offer the short stories "Mother of a Queen," "The Light of the World," and "An Homage to Switzerland" to Perkins at cut rate prices in an effort to "bitch cosmo" and take another swipe at Fitzgerald and his writer's block.

In a letter to *Cosmopolitan Magazine* editor Bill Engel sent from the Nordquist Ranch earlier that summer, Hemingway explained the strangeness of the Switzerland story: "This is a damned good story—3 stories in one. The amount of dialogue makes it long in space. It's a new form for a story. The fact that all three parts open the same way or practically the same is intentional and is supposed to represent Switzerland metaphysically."[15] The story ends with the main character revealing to a stranger who remarks that he would like to meet his father:

> "I'm sure he would of liked to meet you but he died last year. Shot himself, oddly enough."
> "I am very truly sorry. I am sure his loss was a blow to science as well as to his family."
> "Science took it awfully well."[19]

This exchange at the end of "Homage to Switzerland" was the first time Hemingway dealt with his father's suicide in his writing. The line, "Science took it awfully well," indicated that the family didn't.

The rest of Hemingway's letters that year were to friends and critics. The letters to friends were long and sincere, while his letters to critics were short, scathing, and often hilarious. It was from the L—T Ranch that he answered Paul Romaine's famous charge that he was obsessed with "Lost generations and bulls." Hemingway wrote:

I wrote, in 6 weeks, one book about a few drunks and to show the superiority of the earlier Hebrew writers over the later quoted Ecclesiastes versus G. Stein. This was some seven years ago. Since then have not been occupied with this so-called (but not by me) Lost Generation. About Bulls—for ten years or so bullfighting was my recreation and amusements...I wrote a book to clear them up and keep them - also something about Spain which I know a little about having lived there. I have to live sometimes and I have quite a few things to write and my mind is not occupied with lost generations and bulls. The address here is Cooke, Montana."[20]

To the editors of *Hound and Horn,* he wrote a response to their autopsy of Dos Passos, Fitzgerald, and himself. His tongue-in-cheek reply was filled with sexual innuendo and a thinly veiled attack on the masculinity of the article's author, Lawrence Leighton. *Hound and Horn* published the letter in their October-December 1932 edition.[21]

As harsh as Hemingway could be to critics and fellow writers, he was immensely sensitive to criticism of his work. So much so that he left a hunting trip with Thompson, Chub, and John Staebe on Timber Creek in order to check the mail for reviews after the release of *Death in the Afternoon.* During the thirty-mile ride out of Timber Creek, down Crandall Creek, and back up the Clark's Fork toward the L—T, he encountered a moose at close range. Because he lacked a license, he was compelled to leave it alone.[22] Eight years later he would have his character Robert Jordan recall the episode in *For Whom the Bell Tolls.* When he reached the ranch he presented Olive Nordquist with a few sage grouse, made himself a whiskey sour, and sat down to read the reviews. While not overly negative, the reviews were not glowing either. Hemingway was irked enough to reply to Bob Coates of the *New Yorker* immediately:

But I'm damned if I wrote any petulant jabs about Faulkner and the hell with you for telling citizens that I did. All the petulant jabs you like against Waldo Frank (of yourself even, if you're looking for them), or for anyone for whom I have no particular respect. But I

Hemingway poses with two trophy elk racks and the hide of the massive black that he shot. The bear was a good deal larger than the one his friend Charles Thompson had shot, satisfying the author's unquenchable competitiveness.
ERNEST HEMINGWAY COLLECTION. JOHN F. KENNEDY PRESIDENTIAL LIBRARY AND MUSEUM, BOSTON.

have plenty of respect for Faulkner and wish him all the luck. That does not mean I would not joke about him. There are no subjects that I would not jest about if the jest were funny enough. (just as, liking wing shooting, I would shoot my own mother if she went in coveys and had good strong flight.) If it was not funny to you that is my, or perhaps your, hard luck.[23]

While Hemingway was at the ranch with the reviews, Charles Thompson had teamed up with John Staebe to shoot a large black bear. Hemingway was determined to get his own bear. On October 11, he rode with Lawrence Nordquist and Huck Mees to a bear bait up Pilot Creek. Mees was a seasoned mountain man who had entered local folklore with his "first ascent" of Pilot Peak earlier that summer.[24] At dusk a large black bear arrived and began tearing at the rotting horse. Hemingway's first shot sent the wounded bear running into the woods. After following the blood trail through the snow, in the waning light, his second shot brought down the five-hundred-pound bear from twenty feet.[25]

Following a wounded bear into cover at dusk is about as exhilarating and dangerous as hunting gets, and it was just the sort of experience Hemingway was looking for when he settled on the Yellowstone High Country as his North American hunting grounds. The bear was a good deal larger than the one Thompson had shot, satisfying Hemingway's unquenchable competitiveness. They returned to the ranch and feasted on elk and venison while preparing to leave the ranch for that year. On October 14 Hemingway wrote three long letters to some of his closest friends.

To Henry Strater, he explained the Africa postponement and summed up the months hunting with Thompson. In his letter to Guy Hickock, his version of the birth of Gregory showed how Hemingway felt about his family at this time in his life: "Had baby—9 lbs 7 ounces or 19 lbs 17 ounces—Hell of a big baby anyway with gigantic sexual equipment and deep base voice...Well Pauline is cockeyed beautiful—figure lovely after Greg born—never looked nor felt better—Rode hard here all summer—shot and fished—She hunted here for the first 5 days of the season then went down to Key West to work on house."[26] (Ten years later, under his father's guidance, Gregory would tie for first in the Cuban Shooting Championship, beating a former champion of both Cuba and Spain named Cappie Cruz and President Batista's chief of police, among others.)[27]

Later in that same letter Hemingway addressed the effects of the Great Depression creeping into the lives of the Hemingways and their friends. He wrote: "Don't ever come home thinking U.S.A. [is] interesting - It is just the same as ever only now they are all broke where before they were lousy with

*In a letter to a friend, Hemingway described his wife, Pauline, shown here
at one of the cabins on the L—T Ranch, "Well Pauline is cockeyed beautiful – figure lovely after Greg born – never looked or felt better – Rode hard
[h]ere all summer – shot and fished."*
Patrick Hemingway Papers, C0066, Manuscripts Division, Department
of Rare Books and Special Collections, Princeton University Library.

cash. The scene hasn't changed. Just the condition of the actors… Well well well this depression is hell - On the other hand we didn't participate in the boom…Ernest"[28] Having driven from Key West to the Rockies three times in the previous six years, he had seen thousands of unemployed men roaming the highways and railroads, and he had even been treated like one by the children of Piggott, Arkansas. However, he had spent most of the Roaring Twenties in Europe and believed that the excesses of the previous decade had led to the inevitable economic collapse.

The beginning of his letter to Dos Passos continues to highlight the economic situation. After thanking his friend for loaning him one hundred dollars, Hemingway talked about hustling short stories for cash and reminded him of the continuing value of Red Lodge moonshine in the mountains: "By Christ it made me feel good to get your letter. It certainly did…We've been killing meat for Ivan and Chub to get married on. Rode all the way to Timber Creek cabin in a blizzard—read your damned letter over and take a shot of Red Lodge moon to keep warm."

Towards the end of the letter was a rare glimpse into his politics: "I suppose I am an anarchist - but it takes a while to figure out….I don't believe and can't believe in too much government—no matter what good is the end. To hell with the Church when it becomes a state and the hell with the state when it becomes a church. Also it is very possible that tearing down is more important than building up. Well the hell with all this whisker pulling. Chub, Ivan and the Nordquists send you their best as does old Charles. My Love to Kate… So long Dos…Hem."[29] Hemingway's disdain for politics extended to the upcoming election between Roosevelt and Hoover which he considered a contest between "the paralytic demagogue" (Roosevelt) and the "syphilitic baby" (Hoover). While he could catch the occasional campaign speech on his portable radio, he said he "liked the yowling of the coyotes in the hills far better."[30]

With the hunting done and his letters written, Hemingway and Thompson headed to Cooke City for the annual Old Timers Fish Fry. It was an experience he would remember forever. In a piece called "A Paris Letter" for the February, 1934, edition of *Esquire,* he wrote, "The boys who had tried to drag

Bull-Neck Moose-Face, the truck driver, to death the night of the Old Timers' Fish Fry because he was alleged to have hit a lady with a poker, were still in jail." Eighteen years later, in Chapter 5 of *Across the River and into the Trees,* Colonel Cantwell uses this event to settle an argument with Jackson, his driver, as to what constitutes a tough town: "O.K., Jackson. Maybe we move in different circles. Or maybe we have differing definitions of the word. But this town of Venice, with everybody being polite and having good manners, is as tough as Cooke City, Montana, on the day they have the Old Timers' Fish Fry."

On October 16 Hemingway wrote a check to Nordquist for $1,620[31] to cover his stay at the ranch. Then he and Thompson drove away during a blizzard with a candle in a tin can on the dashboard to help defrost the windshield. They stopped in Cody and stayed at the Chamberlin Hotel[32]. The following morning Hemingway mailed off fourteen letters and some final signed page proofs of *Death in the Afternoon* from a Studebaker garage.

Hemingway left the ranch that fall not sure when he would return. In his future lay the uncertainty and danger of the upcoming African safari. In the future of the mountains he had grown to love was a plan to pave a road between Red Lodge and Cooke City. Hemingway was convinced that the road would bring more people and drive all the game into the refuge of Yellowstone National Park. A temporary dam had already ruined one of his favorite fishing streams and road builders searching for gravel had destroyed another one. Because of these changes, Hemingway had hunted, fished, and lived with extra vigor that summer. For these and other reasons, it would be almost four years before Hemingway returned to the Yellowstone High Country.

Hemingway, his rifle slung on his shoulder, poses with elk and mule deer trophies taken in 1932, another banner year for Hemingway in the Yellowstone High Country.
ERNEST HEMINGWAY COLLECTION. JOHN F. KENNEDY PRESIDENTIAL LIBRARY AND MUSEUM, BOSTON.

Hemingway with one of the grizzly bears that he shot in 1936.
ERNEST HEMINGWAY COLLECTION. JOHN F. KENNEDY PRESIDENTIAL LIBRARY AND MUSEUM,
BOSTON.

IV

1936

On August 10, 1936, the Hemingway family returned to the L—T Ranch with unanimous vigor. They moved right into the Sidley Cabin, and Jack and Patrick leaped into action. Jack reacquainted himself with the river where he had learned to fly fish four years earlier, and during his first twelve hours there, Patrick got off his horse only long enough to eat.[1] Glad to be back after nearly four years, Hemingway was at his best at the ranch. He went to work rekindling friendships at the L—T: "He had an appealing zest for life of all forms. He had a particular camaraderie with all of the ranch hands. He would join the children's baseball game in the corral after dinner until dark."[2] The Allington brothers and Ivan Wallace were no longer employed at the ranch, but Chub Weaver was happy to come over from Red Lodge to spend another few months with the Hemingways, who paid him $75 a month for his role as "cook, factotum, and outdoor instructor for the young."[3] Patrick Hemingway remembered Chub this way in a 1999 documentary for Montana PBS:

Chub Weaver was my Godfather and when I was seven or eight years old my dad and my mother went on this pack trip to hunt grizzlies. Chub went along as the cook and of course I and Chub were sort of left alone in camp when everybody went out to look at the baits or hunt elk or whatever they were doing. I'd been backwards in learning to read and so my parents brought along the reader that I was learning from and Chub said 'Oh well I'll teach him to read. That's

Hemingway sits in front of grizzly bear hides and beside a trophy elk rack with his life-long friend Chub Weaver. Weaver was a hunting guide who was also known as a good camp cook.
ERNEST HEMINGWAY COLLECTION. JOHN F. KENNEDY PRESIDENTIAL LIBRARY AND MUSEUM, BOSTON.

a good thing because I haven't got anything to do while you're out.' He was just wonderful. He just really got me interested and by the end of that pack trip I was reading.[4]

That Hemingway chose Chub Weaver to be godfather to his second son illustrates how important this part of the world and the people in it had become to him. Considering that the godparents to his first son, Bumby, were lesbian lovers Gertrude Stein and Alice Toklas from the Roaring Twenties' Paris, the fact that Chub Weaver—a hunting guide, camp cook, and occasional bootlegger from Red Lodge, Montana—was given the same role to Hemingway's second son illustrates Hemingway's deep appreciation of people from all walks of life and his ability to comfortably exist among them.

Surrounded by his family and old friends in the now comfortable confines of the Yellowstone High Country, Hemingway described his return to the ranch in a letter to Arnold Gingrich:

> Since we've been out here I've written little over thirty thousand words. A big part of the time have been in a bell epoque. Have only laid off to go down to hunt antelope for three days and three days up to the Granites to fish out of, say, thirty-six days. Caught 6 over 16 inches (rainbows) 4 over 18 inch in the Granites. The book is 3⁄4 through, nearly, and can see the end….Finished the section I'm doing today and am riding up to hunt tomorrow for three days. Maybe five. When come back will be full of juice again but am taking yellow paper and pencil along in case it should snow or had what couldn't wait."[5]

The novel this time was *To Have and Have Not*, which he finished that year at the ranch. Between the 1932 visit and the 1936 visit, Hemingway had published *Green Hills of Africa*, a nonfiction account of his first trip to Africa. It wasn't too popular with the public or the critics, but his friend John Staebe gets a mention and, as it was a hunting novel, Hemingway reminisced about his experience in the Yellowstone High Country several times, comparing the landscapes, habits of the game, and the guides from the two continents.

It was, however, the short stories that Hemingway wrote that defined this period. Along with "The Gambler, the Nun and the Radio," his account of his hospital stay in Billings, he published "A Clean, Well-Lighted Place" and "An Homage to Switzerland," which both show Hemingway's attempt to exercise the demons of his father's suicide through his typewriter. Other stories included "Wine of Wyoming," set in Sheridan, Wyoming, during his first venture west in 1928; "The Natural History of the Dead," penned in cabin number one of the L—T in 1930; "The Light of the World," written at the ranch in

1932; and "Fathers and Sons," one of his more poignant stories. These were all published in *Winner take Nothing*, his third collection of short stories and they all depended, in one way or another, on his time outside of Yellowstone.

In "Fathers and Sons," Hemingway re-introduced his alter ego Nick Adams, only Nick is no longer a boy. In the story, Nick is grown and has a son who asks him why they never visit Nick's father's grave. At one point the young boy asks his father if he could be buried at a convenient place so the child could visit him after he dies. After some discussion, Nick Adams' son suggests, "Couldn't we all be buried out at the ranch."[6]

In early 1936 "The Snows of Kilimanjaro" was published. It came to be regarded as one of Hemingway's greatest efforts. The story was about a writer named Harry dying of gangrene within view of the great African mountain. It includes several hallucinatory reflections that the writer claimed could have comprised four novels. One of these passages was about the writer's times at "the ranch" and his neglect of those memories as material:

> But what about the rest that he had never written? What about the ranch and the silvered gray of the sage brush, the quick, clear water in the irrigation ditches, and the heavy green of the alfalfa. The trail went up into the hills and the cattle in the summer were shy as deer. The bawling and the steady noise and slow moving mass raising a dust as you brought them down in the fall. And behind the mountains, the clear sharpness of the peak in the evening light and, riding down along the trail in the moonlight, bright across the valley. Now he remembered coming down through the timber in the dark holding the horse's tail when you could not see and all the stories that he meant to write….He knew at least twenty good stories from out there and he'd never written one, why?[7]

From here Hemingway, as though to prove he had these stories in his head, had the dying writer tell the tale of the murder of Jim Smith, the original owner of the ranch. Smith was shot by Tony Rodoscheck on April 1, 1912, at the L—T in a dispute over hay. Jim Smith Peak sits eight miles outside of Yellowstone's Northeast Entrance in the heart of Hemingway country. The writer included himself in the action and never mentioned anyone by name, but the story is unmistakable because of the circumstances surrounding Smith's death. [8]

Between his hallucinations, the dying writer berates a woman who sounds a lot like Pauline. The abuse is merciless and very personal, much of it stemming from guilt the writer feels from the woman's superior wealth. Pauline's uncle had purchased the Hemingways' Key West house and car, and funded Hemingway's Africa trip. To fuel the paranoia, anger, and bitterness of Harry, Hemingway also tapped into his experience at the Billings hospital in 1930. For five weeks Pauline had stayed at Hemingway's bedside while he recovered from his badly broken arm. After infections, unsuccessful surgeries, sleepless nights, and constant morphine, to call Hemingway irritable would have been a gross understatement. All this, along with the fear of losing the use of his writing, shooting, and fishing arm, brought out Hemingway's resentment in full, and many of the Hemingway's close friends began to feel more sorry for Pauline than for her husband. While this aspect of his hospital experience didn't make it into "The Gambler, the Nun and the Radio," it seems to have manifested itself in "The Snows of Kilimanjaro."

This story is also famous for a dig at F. Scott Fitzgerald as Harry refers to the "poor Scott Fitzgerald" and considers him ruined. Hemingway and Fitzgerald's friendship had been strained for a few years because of a feud between Hemingway and Fitzgerald's wife, Zelda. Hemingway felt his father had been dominated by his mother, Grace. Clarence Hemingway's inability to stand up to her, Ernest believed, led to his father's suicide. There seems to have been a similar relationship between Fitzgerald and Zelda, and having witnessed the result of that dynamic in his parents, Hemingway seemed to blame Zelda for Fitzgerald's shortcomings. Until the publication of "Snows," all of Hemingway's criticism of Fitzgerald had been in private.

In *Green Hills of Africa,* which was published earlier that year, Hemingway also took a swipe at old friend Gertrude Stein, and that spring he had a fist fight with the poet Wallace Stevens. It seemed that in the summer of 1936,

Hemingway was at war with the whole literary world. Many of these conflicts, and others as well, found their way into *To Have and Have Not,* as he worked incessantly to finish the book before leaving the L—T.

The other war in Hemingway's life that summer was the Spanish Civil War. Spain was close to his heart, having lived there, written two books about it, and having seen the seeds of war when he was there finalizing *Death in the Afternoon.* The war had just started, and though he felt he should be there, another trip to the Yellowstone High Country was deemed more important for the family, for the hunting and fishing, and most importantly for finishing his next novel. In a letter sent from Cooke City to Maxwell Perkins dated September 26, 1936, he wrote: "Hope to finish my first draft this month i.e. October. If I go to Spain will see you in NY on my way through. I hate to have missed this Spanish thing worse than anything in the world but have to have this book finished first."[9] Hemingway would give the next two years of his life to the Loyalist cause in Spain, but for now his focus was on finishing *To Have and Have Not.*

In early September, Tom and Lorraine Shevlin arrived for a visit. The Hemingways and the Shevlins took a trip to Granite Lake to fish and then headed down country to hunt pronghorn antelope. Everything, it seems, was going well until Hemingway gave Tom a draft of his new novel to read. Tom, while aware of his friend's sensitivity to criticism, told Hemingway he liked some parts of the book, including the main character, but disliked other parts. At this point, Hemingway angrily "pitched the manuscript out of the window into a bank of early snow."[10]

The two didn't speak for a couple of days until Hemingway apologized for his temper and directed his attention to a bear bait that Lawrence Nordquist had placed up Timber Creek. Even though this was his third extended trip to the Yellowstone High Country, Hemingway had never shot a grizzly bear and desperately wanted to. The Shevlins made camp up Timber Creek while the Hemingways took 12-year-old Jack to Cody and saw him off to school in Chicago. Ernest, Pauline, and Patrick then headed back to meet up with their friends, along with Chub and Nordquist. Late that afternoon

Hemingway poses with his son Patrick by the grizzly bear Hemingway killed near the confluence of Crandall and Timber creeks.
ERNEST HEMINGWAY COLLECTION. JOHN F. KENNEDY PRESIDENTIAL LIBRARY AND MUSEUM, BOSTON.

Hemingway poses with the hides of the three grizzly bears that he and his friend Tom Shevlin shot in September 1936.
Ernest Hemingway Collection. John F. Kennedy Presidential Library and Museum, Boston.

Hemingway walked toward the bait with Lorraine while her husband covered them from an adjacent hillside. Tom Shevlin saw the grizzlies leave the bait and head toward Hemingway and Lorraine. Too far away to warn them, Shevlin's nerves were settled when he heard all the shooting as "Papa could shoot a 30.06 like a machine gun."[11] Hemingway described the hunt in a letter to Perkins:

> Last six days hunted Grizzlies and we got three and two good Elk. Tom Shevlin got one and I got two out of three that I ran onto in the last timber up near timberline while hunting Elk. It was very exciting. Tommy got his two days later on a bait. I could have killed the three but they were so damned handsome I was sorry I killed

more than the one but at the time did not have much time to decide. There is one very huge one that has been killing cattle that was so big that the Govt hunter when he ran onto him was afraid to shoot that am going after in about ten days. Am back to work now. Have never shot better. Hope I can write as well. Have some 55,000 some words done. It has gone very well lately."[12]

Another of Hemingway's best short stories, "The Short Happy life of Francis Macomber," was published in 1936. It is the story of a safari in eastern Africa in which a man and his wife hunt dangerous game with a great white hunter. Whether Hemingway's encounter with the three grizzly bears could have been the inspiration for this famous story is debatable. It is known that years later Hemingway told the grizzly bear story to his friend and biographer A. E. Hotchner and claimed that Lorraine Shevlin was the inspiration for Margot Macomber. Hemingway also claimed to have shot all three of the grizzlies and describes Lorraine as "emerging from his behind" after the action.[13] Hotchner met Hemingway in 1948 and knew him until his death, so Hemingway's re-telling of the bear hunt was between twelve and thirty years after it happened. It smacked of machismo and bravado with Hemingway exaggerating the circumstances. This was a very different account than the one he offered Perkins just days after the hunt in which he regretted shooting more than one of the bears on account of their beauty. Perhaps the different stories illustrated how "Hemingway in the Yellowstone High Country" changed into the "bigger-than-life Hemingway" the world came to know.

"The Short Happy Life of Francis Macomber" was first written as "A Budding Friendship" in the spring of 1936. While most scholars agree that Jane and Grant Mason were used as inspiration for the Macombers, perhaps the Shevlins played a part. They had spent time with Hemingway in Bimini that same spring, and Hemingway did not have a lot of respect for Tom Shevlin as a hunter: "Tommy shot a doe and missed seven bucks sitting. His wife is still missing them. He is, as you know, a nice kid but he can't shoot. He has known so many big game hunters that he became a big game hunter without

*Pauline and Patrick Hemingway, Tom and Lorraine Shevlin, and Ernest Hemingway pose
with Shevlin's large grizzly bear taken up Timber Creek.*
ERNEST HEMINGWAY COLLECTION. JOHN F. KENNEDY PRESIDENTIAL LIBRARY AND MUSEUM,
BOSTON.

ever burning the necessary cartridges."[14] All of Hemingway's friends and their
wives ran the risk of ending up as material in his work.

"The Short Happy Life of Francis Macomber" appeared in *Cosmopolitan*
magazine in September, the same time that Hemingway was hunting grizzly
bears with the Shevlins in Wyoming. With his only shooting of a grizzly and
the publication of the story happening virtually simultaneously, it is easy to see
how Hemingway always saw the two events as connected. After the hunt, the
Shevlins and the Hemingways dined on bear meat at Ernest's insistence. "The
meat was rank and stringy, cooked middling rare, and eaten in the form of
sandwiches made with sourdough pancakes spread with orange marmalade."[15]

Hemingway had finally shot a grizzly; in fact, he had shot two. But the fact
remained that Tom Shevlin's bear was the biggest. On the ride back to the
L—T, suffering from an acute case of wounded pride, Hemingway bet the

younger, lighter Shevlin $500 that he could beat him in a horse race over the final five miles to the ranch. Shevlin pulled ahead in the final stretch, splattering the writer with so much mud that it had to be removed with trowels over several hours. In an effort to even the score, Hemingway challenged Shevlin to an evening game of craps and promptly lost $900.

In a matter of days, Shevlin had shot a bigger grizzly, won a horse race and crap game, and panned Hemingway's new novel. After describing this episode in a letter to his friend Archie MacLeish, Hemingway remarked darkly: "Me I like life very much. So much it will be a big disgust when have to shoot myself. Maybe pretty soon I guess, although will arrange to be shot in order not have bad effect on kids. Going to finish this book. Got to get to work now."[16]

About Hemingway, Shevlin later said: "It's extraordinary the number of times he mentioned suicide. The picture of Hemingway as the very tough, almost bloodthirsty character, because of his hunting and love of bullfighting, is very exaggerated. He was very, very intelligent and read copiously. He was a complex, very difficult man with a tremendous zest for life and when he did anything he did it absolutely up to the hilt, no half measures."[17]

After the Shevlins left the ranch, Hemingway went back to work on *To Have and Have Not* and continued his correspondence with F. Scott Fitzgerald. He was also corresponding with Marjorie Kinnan Rawlings (*The Yearling*), another Scribner's author he respected and who shared a friendship with Fitzgerald. He had written to her from the L—T Ranch earlier that summer: "Lately I have felt I was going to die in a short time (hope that is nuts and that live to be a wise old man with white beard and chew tobacco)...."[18] Rawlings went to visit Fitzgerald in North Carolina in October, and they eventually began to discuss Hemingway. Fitzgerald compared Ernest's mention of him in "The Snows of Kilimanjaro" to "giving an uppercut to some harmless weakling" and Rawlings suggested that it was some sort of "'sadistic maladjustment' that made him go around knocking people down." At the very moment his peers were conducting a deep psychoanalysis of him in North Carolina, Hemingway was busy at the ranch trying to trap a pack rat that had been keeping the family awake in the Sidley Cabin.[19]

The residents of the Yellowstone High Country had never suffered for booze, but with the opening of the Beartooth Highway and the repeal of Prohibition, Cooke City bars were now only a ten-minute drive away. Prohibition ended in 1933 and in 1934 Hoosiers Bar opened, meaning Hemingway would have had drinks there in 1936, 1938, and 1939. Grace Anderson who worked at Hoosiers Motel and Bar in Cooke City in the 1930s, recalled Hemingway coming into the bar mornings or afternoons. "We never closed," she said. "He'd sit at the end of the bar and push his glass across the bar when he wanted another drink. He was not one to visit; we had the impression he was there to write his books and didn't want to bother with anyone."[20] Her memories of Hoosiers in the 1930s mirror Hemingway's description of The Index Bar in "A Man of the World": "Then The Index was open all night long and got the early morning trade from daylight until ten o'clock, in the morning the drinks were on the house. They were the only saloons in Jessup and they did not have to do that sort of thing. But that was the way they were."[21] "A Man of the World" was published in 1957 in the 100th anniversary issue of *The Atlantic Monthly*. It was Hemingway's last story that was published in his lifetime. While people at the L—T all had good things to say about Hemingway and his family, the people of Cooke City were less enamored. Jon Fryer remembered that his mother, who taught at the Cooke City School in the twenties and thirties, used one phrase to describe the general attitude toward Hemingway: "He was roundly disliked."[22]

The ranch, however, provided Hemingway with a complete escape from critics, from politics and war, and from his peers and the pressures they put on him. While he was in the mountains, he was concerned with only three things: his family, his work, and the woods. That year was another vintage year for Hemingway. He had shot his first grizzly bear, along with elk, antelope, and grouse. He had good fishing with Pauline and the boys, and he was able to rekindle friendships with the Nordquists, John Staebe, and especially Chub Weaver. Most importantly, this visit to the ranch enabled him to finish another novel. He had written 55,000 words or roughly 350 pages of *To Have and Have Not* since arriving in July.

Nonetheless, some of the shine on Hemingway's private wilderness was fading. Fire had burned a lot of his favorite hunting ground and the Beartooth Highway had been completed between Red Lodge and Cooke City. The highway, an engineering marvel that spanned 63 miles between the two Montana towns and crossed the Beartooth Pass at nearly 11,000 feet, was part of FDR's effort to put the country to work during the Depression. In Hemingway's mind it was just an intrusion into the wilderness he loved. After returning to the Irati River in Spain and finding that river, which had been so much a part of *The Sun Also Rises,* ruined by logging, Hemingway felt that the Clark's Fork was under the same pressure. He also feared that all the big game would be driven into the refuge of Yellowstone National Park.

After leaving the ranch that fall, Hemingway turned his attention to Spain. The civil war was already under way so Hemingway almost immediately made arrangements to go there. After a brief stop in Paris to drink with friends at the Hotel Montana, he made his way to already besieged Madrid. At this point, Hemingway considered himself an anti-war correspondent mostly interested in keeping America out of the approaching war in Europe and commenting on the effect of civil war on the ordinary people of the countryside. It wasn't until his old friend and artist Luis Quintanilla told him of the destruction of all his frescoes by Franco's fascist "rebels" that Hemingway's position on the war began to form. Quintanilla had been imprisoned in the early 1930s, and Hemingway and Dos Passos had worked to ensure his release. Ironically, when Quintanilla laid down his paintbrush and picked up a rifle, his first act as a Spanish Loyalist was to storm the Montana barracks, the very prison the two writers had sprung him from years earlier.

The storming of the barracks signaled the onset of the Spanish Civil War. While Hemingway and fellow war correspondent and future wife Martha Gellhorn had trouble getting into the country as neutral correspondents, Italy's Mussolini landed 12,000 fascist troops in southern Spain. Hemingway would not remain neutral for long.

When Hemingway returned to the L—T Ranch in 1938 after a four-year absence, people at the ranch noticed, "He had filled out physically in appearance. He had suffered and matured."
ERNEST HEMINGWAY COLLECTION. JOHN F. KENNEDY PRESIDENTIAL LIBRARY AND MUSEUM, BOSTON.

V

1938

Hemingway, Pauline, and Patrick returned to the ranch in early August 1938. His time in Spain had changed him emotionally and the years had changed him physically. People at the ranch noticed: "He had filled out physically in appearance. He had suffered and matured."[1]

While the Spanish Civil War wouldn't end officially until April 1939, Nationalist General Francisco Franco had already called for the Loyalists to surrender, and after their defeat at the Battle of Ebro in 1938, the Loyalist army fell apart. By the time Hemingway arrived at the L—T, the war was lost. He had been out of the United States for most of the last two years and was craving the American West and time with his family.

In addition to his work as a war correspondent, Hemingway had been writing articles for a magazine called *KEN*. His association with the magazine was risky since it was known for its communist sympathies, but after his time in Spain, he had decided that no matter what the political cost, he was firmly on the side of the Spanish Loyalists and their communist backers. In his view, it was Hitler and Mussolini and their backers, including the Catholic Church, who presented the greatest threat to Europe, America, and the artist way of life. Earlier, in a 1932 letter to Dos Passos sent from the ranch, Hemingway had remarked, "To hell with the Church when it becomes a state and the hell with the state when it becomes a church."[2] This was exactly what had happened in Spain. Spain had the most top heavy church hierarchy in the world (aside from Tibet), and the clergy was paid very well by the state.[3] Hemingway felt that the

Catholic Church had betrayed the Spanish people by siding with the fascists, and he blamed America and England for not doing more to help. Hemingway was a man known for many things, but first and foremost he was a writer and artist. Shortly before heading west in 1938, he addressed the Writers Congress at Carnegie Hall in the only public speech of his career:

> Really good writers are always rewarded under almost any existing system of government that they can tolerate. There is only one form of government that cannot produce good writers, and that system is fascism. For fascism is a lie told by bullies. A writer who will not lie cannot live and work under fascism. [4]

The family set out from Key West on August 4, and the trip was eventful. They had to stop a few hours into the trip after Hemingway scratched his eye, and then they ran out of money in Denver and had to have Max Perkins wire money to get them the rest of the way. Hemingway and Pauline argued most of the trip while Patrick rode in the back. To add to the difficulties they already had, Hemingway's new distaste for the Catholic Church clashed with Pauline's Catholicism.

As the rain beat down in the Clark's Fork Valley, Hemingway went to work arranging the stories for his upcoming anthology, which was to be a combination of all of his previously published short stories and some newer unpublished works, including *The Fifth Column*, his first and only attempt at playwriting. After struggling for a few days, he decided on the order that would be most effective and sent it off to Perkins:

> That is the order that after reading them all over and thinking it over I believe to be the soundest and would like to go on unless you have objections to it...in making a book of short stories readable there is a hell of a lot to having them placed properly in relation to each other. Will now go ahead on the preface. It's raining here and snowing higher up...no time to write Max. Must get busy on the Preface. I think it will make a fine book, really. [5]

The preface, although short, provided insight into how Hemingway went about his writing. He claimed that the necessity of experiencing what he intended to write about could actually inhibit his ability to write until, working constantly, his skills would come back to him, allowing him to fully experience his subject matter and to convey that experience while at the peak of his powers:

> In going where you have to go, and doing what you have to do, and seeing what you have to see, you dull and blunt the instrument you write with. But I would rather have it bent and dull and know I had to put it on the grindstone again and hammer it into shape and put a whetstone to it, and know that I had something to write about, than to have it bright and shining and nothing to say, or smooth and well-oiled in the closet, and unused. Now it is necessary to get to the grindstone again."[6]

Also in the preface, he provided the first published indication of the value of the Yellowstone High Country as a place to work: "Beside *The Fifth Column*, I wrote...part of *The Sun Also Rises* and the first third of *To Have and Have Not* in Madrid. It was a good place for working. So were Key West, Florida, in the cool months; [and] the ranch near Cooke City, Montana...."[7]

With the preface complete and sent off, Hemingway worked on preparing *The Fifth Column* for publication. *The Fifth Column* represented one of Hemingway's only major failures. He had intended for it to be performed on Broadway, but circumstance and perhaps the play's inadequacy prevented this from happening. One potential producer died and another ran out of money as America struggled to emerge from the Great Depression. Like all of his new work at the time, the play centered on the Spanish Civil War. After its failure as a play, he struggled to reshape it in order to squeeze it into the "first forty-nine book." Polly Copeland, a resident of the ranch at the time, remembered this period:

Every now and then, Pauline Hemingway would pick wild strawberries in the woods on a late afternoon, which she would brew with gin, powdered sugar and lemon, making a powerful drink that we would be invited to sip, sitting on the cabin steps, looking up to the glorious sunset color radiating over Beartooth Butte while Ernest Hemingway would read to us his latest chapter on the 'The Fifth Column.' On those nights we would arrive at the ranch dinner very late, but thrilled over hearing Ernest Hemingway read from his heart.[8]

Perhaps Hemingway knew in his heart that this would be the only time that anyone would hear *The Fifth Column* performed. As the Yellowstone High Country became more and more of an inspiration for his writing, it became harder for him to do the more mundane work of his profession there. The ordering of already written stories into compilations and the writing of prefaces was not the type of work he went to the ranch to do, and the last thing he wanted to do that summer was rewrite the play that had given him "nothing but trouble for seven or eight months." On August 3, the day before he left Key West, Hemingway had remarked that he was "heartily sick of his play" and "he wanted to get it behind him in favor of other projects."[9]

After he had sent everything off to Perkins for *The First Forty-nine Stories*, he had effectively given up on his play. With steady rain preventing any meaningful fishing, Hemingway set to work on his Spanish Civil War stories. Since leaving the ranch in late 1936, he had spent most of his time in Spain reporting on the war, completing fifteen magazine articles, and filing $15,000 worth of newspaper correspondences[10]. He had also spent a lot of time on his play and written "The Old Man at the Bridge" for inclusion in the short story compilation, but the real stories of his time in Spain were still in his head. The time at the ranch was the perfect opportunity to put them to paper.

In those two years there had also been major developments in Hemingway's personal life. His relationships with Fitzgerald and Stein were essentially over, and his friendship with Dos Passos had become strained over their disagreements concerning the war and the fate of their friend Jose Robles at the hands of Russian intelligence. The Richard Gordon character in *To Have and Have Not* was also a matter of contention between the two writers. Gordon was loosely based on Dos Passos, and the writer was not flattered by the portrayal. Another of Hemingway's literary friends, Tom Wolfe, had died that summer.

The most significant change in his personal life was his relationship with war correspondent Martha Gellhorn. They had met in Key West in 1936 and were together in Spain. It was a relationship that would eventually end his marriage to Pauline. After completing the preface to *The First Forty-nine Stories* and sending it to his editor, Hemingway had included a dedication to fellow war correspondents with whom he had worked in Spain. It was written in longhand (probably added after Pauline had proofread the work): "To Marty and Herbert with Love." The dedication never appeared in the book.

Even at the ranch, people knew of the brewing romance. One visitor recalled, "Once I told Ernest that on the winter before, in Chicago, at the Friday Club, I had been much impressed by a lecture about the Spanish Civil War, given by a beautiful, blond reporter named Martie Gellhorn. Ernest looked at me with bright laughing eyes, shaking his head, saying, 'Great girl, Martie, great girl!'"[11]

There were changes at the ranch as well. Olive and Lawrence Nordquist divorced in July, shortly before the Hemingways arrived. Lawrence was granted the L—T Ranch and Olive was awarded their property in Cooke City, where she lived until 1983. Lawrence married his niece and camp cook Irma Patrick and went on to build several properties in Cooke City, later competing with his ex-wife in the hotel business. Ernest and Pauline were close friends with the Nordquists and their divorce must have been unsettling. The dissolution of the Nordquist and Hemingway marriages at the same time led to local speculation about a liaison between Ernest and Olive, but it seems Lawrence's affair with Irma Patrick and Ernest's with Martha Gellhorn led to the two divorces.

Elsewhere in the valley, the opening of the Beartooth Highway had caused a building boom in Cooke City and a new town between Cooke City and the park boundary called Silver Gate was growing. Silver Gate's main attraction was a large hotel called the Gorham Chalet, which opened in 1938. Ralph

Nelles helped build the Chalet and stayed to tend the bar in 1938 and 1939. He later wrote:

> On Saturday nights, Ernest and his wife would come to the Chalet for dinner and to do some dancing. You see we had the only dance band in that area. Ernest was a very heavy drinker and always wanted to stay until we closed the bar. In those days, the county seat, Livingston, Park County, was 110 miles from the Chalet, so we set our own hours when to open the bar and when to close. In those two summers, Ernest did not miss any Saturday nights."[13]

Besides his obligations to Scribner's and to Max Perkins, Hemingway also had a working relationship with *Esquire* magazine and was good friends with the magazine's editor, Arnold Gingrich. *Esquire, Cosmopolitan, Vogue* and *The Atlantic Monthly* all provided places to test out stories and earn money between major projects. After a month writing at the L—T, he wrote to Gingrich: "Enclosed is the story…Christ it is fine to write again and not have to write pieces. I was really going nuts with that. Every time I would get going I would have to interrupt. Now I have another swell story done that only need to go over (maybe the best ever wrote, anyway one of them.) and two chapters done on new novel.[14] The story was "Night Before Battle" and the new novel was *For Whom the Bell Tolls.* "The Denunciation" and "The Butterfly and the Tank" were also crafted that fall and appeared respectively in the 1938 November and December editions of *Esquire.* "Night Before Battle" was published in the February 1939 edition. All three stories take place at Chicote's in Madrid, a bar Hemingway frequented while covering the war. The stories give an indication of the tensions on both sides and how close one was to death at all times. Upon reading "The Butterfly and the Tank," American author John Steinbeck called it "one of the very few finest stories in all time" and considered it so superbly written that it was "almost too much."[15]

For Whom the Bell Tolls is set in the mountains of Spain, and its hero Robert Jordan is from Red Lodge, Montana. Jordan regularly flashes back to his life in

Montana and these flashbacks lean heavily on Hemingway's actual experiences in the mountains around the L—T. While he never wrote a novel about the American West, *For Whom the Bell Tolls* shows the importance of the Yellowstone High County in his work. References to the area are littered throughout the novel, but it is towards the end, at the story's most important and dramatic parts, that the importance of the experiences in the mountains to both Hemingway and Robert Jordan are fully revealed.

As Jordan hangs under the bridge tying off the dynamite during the novel's climax, Hemingway allows him a moment to look down at the stream rushing below: "As he looked a trout rose for some insect and made a circle on the surface...."[16] The horse that whisks Jordan's lover Maria to safety has a white face[17] much like Old Bess, Hemingway's favorite horse at the ranch. The horse that carries Jordan to his fate is clumsy and gray much like Hemingway's least favorite horse at the ranch, Goofy.[18] The wound that Jordan suffers is similar to the one Hemingway suffered in 1930. Although Hemingway broke his arm and Jordan his leg, the details were similar. As Jordan examines his leg "his hands both felt the sharp bone where it pressed against the skin."[19] In describing his broken arm in a letter to Guy Hickock from the Billings Hospital, Hemingway had written, "You could see the point of the bone under the skin, but a compound fracture was avoided."[20] As Jordan lies dying but must try to stay awake, his first instinct is to "Think about Montana."[21] The natural description in the book's closing passages, while an accurate depiction of the mountainous regions of Spain, could just as well describe the area around the ranch: "Then he looked up at the sky. There were big white clouds in it. He touched the palm of his hand against the pine needles where he lay and he touched the bark of the pine trunk that he lay behind."[22] Finally, there is the book's last line as Jordan aims his rifle, "He could feel his heart beating against the pine needle floor of the forest." How many times had Hemingway had that same feeling while hunting in the country surrounding the ranch?

When the North American Newspaper Alliance asked Hemingway to go back to Europe to cover the inevitable onset of World War II, Hemingway was happy to go and, surprisingly, Pauline was happy to let him. Space apart was perhaps what they needed, and they had had none of it since leaving Key West. While Hemingway headed east, Pauline and Patrick stayed behind at the ranch and waited for Toby Bruce to come and pick them up.

This was the first year that Hemingway did not write long accounts of his hunting exploits. There were no laundry lists of fish caught or birds shot, no descriptions of "the heaving chests" of game in his sights, and no letters imploring friends to come and join him. This was Hemingway's shortest trip to the ranch, and rain fell steadily that summer. On the Clark's Fork, one day of rain can muddy the river for a few days, but steady rain can affect the fishing for weeks or even months. The completion of the Beartooth Highway was something else that bothered Hemingway. He had stayed away during its construction and was bitter about the invasion of roads and industry into his favorite fishing grounds. Hemingway felt similarly about a new road to his other home, Key West, saying it was "a tacit invitation to 'every son of a bitch who had ever read a line' of Hemingway to come and be entertained."[23] He feared the Beartooth Highway would forever change another place he had grown to love.

VI

1939

After leaving the Yellowstone High Country in the fall of 1938, Hemingway worked furiously on *For Whom the Bell Tolls*. His marriage to Pauline was in shambles. She knew of his liaisons with Martha Gellhorn in Spain. As Hemingway and Gellhorn's relationship intensified, Gellhorn found a property for them in Cuba. *Finca Vigia* would become Hemingway's home and a place to write for the next twenty-two years. In July 1939 Hemingway was desperate to finish his novel, but Cuba's unbearable heat had slowed his momentum. He wrote Perkins: "It is very hot now and in spite of bragging about how the heat does not affect me I know it is very hot. I got a little stale a week ago so knocked off and spent 3 days at sea. If it gets too hot will go to the ranch and take the children."[1]

A week later, he decided to go to the ranch. At this point Hemingway was burning to finish his novel, keenly aware of the turmoil in Europe and the impending war, and intent on ending his marriage with Pauline. In spite of all this, or perhaps because of it, Hemingway again made a trip to the Yellowstone High Country his priority. In a letter to his first wife, Hadley, he explained:

> Have been working so hard on this novel that could not make any summer plans....Now I know I can't finish it before September First and want so much to have part of the Summer that am going to knock off sometime in August wherever I am and get in some time at the ranch with Bumby and get the other children out there too.

The hand-written caption on this photo demonstrates Hemingway's intimate knowledge of the mountains around Yellowstone National Park's northeast entrance. The caption reads, "Looking up toward Amphitheater Mountain from Soda Butte."
ERNEST HEMINGWAY COLLECTION. JOHN F. KENNEDY PRESIDENTIAL LIBRARY AND MUSEUM, BOSTON.

They had counted and hoped so for the ranch this summer too....So you can figure on sending Bumby to L-T Ranch-Cooke City P.O. Montana when you leave. He knows how to get there. Through the Park to Cooke City. Or via the new road (don't know if it is finished yet) from Cody up the Clarks Fork."[2]

On July 21, 1939, Hemingway turned 40. In a letter to Pauline's mother, he remarked that his birthday had little significance, but his other letters at the time revealed that the turmoil in the world at large and especially the turmoil in his personal life was affecting him. Within a week of his fortieth birthday, Hemingway wrote two letters to Hadley, whom he had not seen in ten years. The main reason was to discuss Jack's future, but Hemingway and Hadley also shared something darker: both of their fathers had committed suicide. Ten years after Clarence Hemingway's suicide, five days after his fortieth birthday, with his marriage on the rocks and the world on the brink of war, Hemingway wrote to his first wife: "Life is quite complicated. And you don't always have luck. Anyway not a thing to write about. Important thing for me is to not get discouraged and take the easy way out like yours and my noted ancestors. Because very bad example to children. Also have to finish this book...."[3] Two days later he wrote a letter to Pauline's parents expressing his sadness about the suicide of a mutual friend who had flown for the Loyalists in Spain: "Was sorry I did not see Frank Tinker before he took such a drastic step. Have argued myself out of that so often that I think I could have kicked the idea out of his head."[4] In a postscript he gave an account of his work and of his desire to head to the mountains: "...have to get back to work now. Been at it every day...for about twelve months now. Machine holding up all right but been going under forced draft for a long time. Think I'd better take it up into the mountains and let it cool off."[5]

In the letter to Pauline's parents, Hemingway maintained that he was working toward 70,000 words on the novel. He had always believed that writing clearly about the most difficult things in life was key to his work. The death of his father had haunted him throughout his time at the L—T; now it was time to put the issue on paper. In Chapter 30 of *For Whom the Bell Tolls,* Robert Jordan remembers riding horses over the Beartooth Mountains with his friend Chub and pausing at a high-country lake. After dismounting, Jordan walks over to a rock outcropping at the edge of the lake, which is rumored to be very deep. Jordan leans over the water, peers at his own reflection, and drops in the Smith and Wesson revolver that his father had used to commit suicide, watching it sink until it is out of sight. As the two ride away from the lake, readers are given this exchange:

> "I know why you did that with the old gun, Bob." Chub said.
> "Well, then we don't have to talk about it then," he had said.
> They never talked about it and that was the end of Grandfather's side arms..."[6]

Chub Weaver later told his son Tom that this scene actually happened just as Hemingway described it in *For Whom the Bell Tolls*. The location was Froze-to-Death Lake on the Beartooth Plateau.[7]

For Robert Jordan, the dropping of the gun represented the rejection of his father's cowardice and the acceptance of his fate and the heroism required to carry out the tasks ahead of him. For Hemingway, it was just as important but not so straightforward. He had never known how he felt about his father's death. He blamed his mother as much as his father, and he felt his uncle should have done more to help out his father financially. It was well known that Hemingway's father had been in considerable pain and suffered from depression in the years leading up to his death. Still, it was ultimately his father's own decision and action, and Hemingway had struggled with it throughout his time at the L—T. He had discussed suicide with friends both close and casual during drunken nights around the fire, or in letters and short stories. Now it was time to head back into the Yellowstone High Country to shed the weight of his father's death in literary form.

With arrangements made for Jack, Ernest wrote to Patrick and Gregory at summer camp and arranged for them to meet him at the ranch. In this letter there was another case of Hemingway suggesting a change of scenery to help re-energize him. It was also an example of the Yellowstone High Country serving as inspiration for his work. He had always valued the area as a place to work and over the years had accrued experiences there that would work their way into several short stories and novels, but none more so than *For Whom the Bell Tolls*. In the letter to Patrick and Gregory, he wrote, "74,000 words done on the new book. I was sitting with prickly heat writing about a snowstorm and it was getting more and more difficult and so I thought 'what the what citizens' let's go out west and see a snowstorm."[8]

With that, Hemingway set off alone for what would be his final visit to the ranch. He was keen to reunite his family at the place that held so many happy memories for all of them, and where he had completed so much good work. Now he set off once more for the Montana-Wyoming border, this time with the nearly finished *For Whom the Bell Tolls*. He was going to write the snowstorm chapter of the novel and tell the tragic story of his grandfather's gun.

Whether Hemingway knew this was going to be his final trip to the ranch is difficult to determine, but clues suggest he did. He knew his marriage to Pauline was essentially over, and every visit to the area had been shared with her. With WWII looming, he knew he would be busy as a war correspondent. He also took great care to make certain that all three of his sons would be there with him. While he never expressly said it was for one last hurrah, that impression was given.

The most telling evidence that Hemingway knew that 1939 would be his last year in the Yellowstone High Country can be found in an essay he wrote for *Vogue* in February 1939. It was entitled, "The Clark's Fork Valley, Wyoming." The essay is written in the past tense and reads like a eulogy of his time in the Yellowstone High Country. He mentions the habits of trout in the river, remembers hunting sheep on the slopes of Pilot and Index peaks in 1930, the grizzlies up Crandall Creek, and the heaving chests of elk and their bugling in the fall. He looks back fondly on his boys learning how to ride horses and on being the first person to bring a car into the valley. As he described his time at the ranch, there is life and death and energy, a vibrancy that symbolized his time in the mountains, but the final paragraph suggests that this chapter of his life was over: "Then there was the winter; the trees bare now, the snow blowing so you could not see, the saddle wet, then frozen as you came down hill...." Hemingway abandoned the past tense only in the final line of the essay. After writing passionately about all of his experiences in retrospect, he ends with, "It's a good country."[9] The sentence essentially implied that it is and always will be good country but for Hemingway, it was over.

The essay reappeared more than sixty years later in *Hemingway on Fishing*. William Kittredge re-affirmed the value of this piece by choosing it to represent Hemingway in his *The Portable Western Reader*, explaining that it "clearly shows Hemingway's style....He shows how significant places connect us to memory."[10]

On his way from Cody to the ranch, Hemingway stopped at a trailhead, turned on his transistor radio, and waited. Hadley, her husband Paul Mowrer, and Jack were staying at a nearby ranch and had taken an afternoon hike to a fishing spot. As they returned, they found Hemingway waiting by their car.

Hemingway never returned to the L—T Ranch after his 1939 trip. Here is one of his backcountry camps from a trip in the Yellowstone High Country.
ERNEST HEMINGWAY COLLECTION. JOHN F. KENNEDY PRESIDENTIAL LIBRARY AND MUSEUM, BOSTON.

After a short meeting, apparently convinced that Hadley and the child they shared were in the best possible hands, Hemingway took Jack up the Clark's Fork to the L—T Ranch.[11] They arrived to find Patrick and Gregory waiting. They settled into the Sidley Cabin by the river. Hemingway would spend his days with the boys and at night retreat to his cabin where "he wrote under his kerosene lamp, late into the night."[12] None of the hands from the early days were at the ranch, but Lawrence Nordquist was still around and Chub Weaver still lived in Red Lodge. The completion of the Beartooth Highway enabled Hemingway to drive to Cooke City, Red Lodge, and even Billings. After these trips he would invariably return with Chub. A local resident remembered, "Several times during his holiday he would drive out over the Beartooth Pass to pick up the latest news from Billings, Montana, 90 miles away. He and his cowboy crony [Chub] would drive back home across the L—T field singing cowboy late in the night."[13]

By 1939, Hemingway and Chub Weaver had been friends for nine years. In chapter 37 of *For Whom the Bell Tolls,* Hemingway paid tribute to their friendship with this passage spoken by the book's main character, Robert Jordan: "I have been all my life in these hills since I have been here. Anselmo is my oldest friend. I know him better than I know Charles, than I know Chub, than I know Guy, than I know Mike, and I know them well."[14] While Anselmo was a fictional character, the rest of the men mentioned were Hemingway's best friends at that time: Charles Thompson, Guy Hickock, Henry 'Mike' Strater, and Leland 'Chub' Weaver.

Work on the novel was interrupted by the outbreak of WWII. Hemingway had the small radio which he had carried with him throughout his time in Spain. As he sat in his cabin on the banks of the Clark's Fork, he was able to keep up with the news from Europe. Fred and Polly Copeland, part owners of the ranch at the time, remembered how they found out the war had started: "On the morning of September 3, 1939, as Fred and I walked across the field to the ranch house for early breakfast, Ernest came running up behind us, saying 'the Germans have marched into Poland! World War II has started, this could not have happened if America had helped in Spain!' Everyone was stunned at the breakfast table over this announcement. Ernest invited us back to his cabin to listen to Hitler ranting and raving to his Nazi cohorts in far off Berlin."[15]

Hemingway had been predicting the war for a couple of years and he knew he would be going to Europe as a war correspondent, but for now, not even the outbreak of war could drag him from the mountains. For the time being he would gather his sons around him, try to finish *For Whom the Bell Tolls,* and bid farewell to the Yellowstone High Country. He knew the war would occupy him for many years to come.

With the war occupying his thoughts and the boys occupying his time, Hemingway was finding it difficult to work. Pauline's arrival in mid-September didn't make things any easier. Hemingway wrote in a letter, "Pauline came home un-expectedly from Europe, got a terrible chest-grippe cold on landing at the Billings Airport and was sick all the time at the ranch. I cooked her meals etc. and tried to take care of her but conditions were primitive and her cold got worse instead of better. The rest you know more about than I do."[16]

By "the rest" he meant the breakup of the Hemingway family that took place at the ranch. Hemingway blamed Pauline's sister Virginia for slandering him and precipitating the breakup. Pauline, however, was well aware of Hemingway's affair with Martha Gellhorn, and while lying sick in bed at the L—T, Pauline made it clear that Hemingway would no longer be welcome at their house in Key West.

As Pauline recovered from her illness, Hemingway stayed at the ranch for what he considered to be an appropriate length of time. Then he arranged for Toby Bruce to drive Pauline and the boys to Piggott and on to Key West, and Hemingway drove by himself to Billings to pick up Martha Gellhorn. The two then headed to the new resort town of Sun Valley, Idaho, where he would finish *For Whom the Bell Tolls*, remain as a summer resident for the next 22 years, and eventually kill himself.

This final visit to the ranch was short, but even in that brief time, Hemingway managed to rendezvous with all three of his children and his first three wives. (He married Gellhorn in December 1940.) He finalized for publication the last of his Spanish Civil War stories, "Under the Ridge," which appeared in *Cosmopolitan* in December 1939, and he did important work on *For Whom the Bell Tolls*. But in September, as leaves on the cottonwoods and aspens began to turn yellow, Ernest Hemingway pulled out of the Yellowstone High Country for the last time.

VII

After He Left

In leaving the Yellowstone High Country that fall, Ernest Hemingway left much of his world behind. He had left Pauline ailing in bed in the middle of nowhere, and because of this, his relationship with his sons would never be the same. While he would continue to see them all periodically, Bumby would go back into the exclusive care of Hadley, and Patrick and Gregory would remain with Pauline. Many of Hemingway's friends were friends of the entire family, and in abandoning Pauline and the boys, Hemingway damaged meaningful relationships with the Thompsons, Murphys, Shevlins, MacLeishs, Mike Strater, and John and Katy Dos Passos. The house in Key West was no longer available to him because it belonged to Pauline's family.

In one climactic period, Hemingway had left behind his two favorite places to write, his favorite hunting and trout fishing country, his wife, his children, his grandfather's gun, and some good friends. He would shoot no more elk, no more sheep, and no more bears. Even fly fishing would no longer play a meaningful part in his life.[1] He would not publish another novel for ten years.

Sun Valley was a new resort town near Ketchum, Idaho. It had been modeled after a Swiss town. In late 1939, many of the chalets, shops, and restaurants were built but still vacant. The owners were touting Sun Valley as a year-round destination: skiing and skating in the winter and fishing and hunting in the summer. Hemingway moved into suite 206 of the luxurious 140-room Sun Valley Lodge and met with the resort's two top publicists the next morning. A lot had changed since the young author first headed deep into the Clark's

Fork Valley to find a primitive place where he could be left alone to write, fish, and hunt. Now he was being commissioned to attract attention to a luxurious playground for the rich and famous.

While Hemingway had yet to match the success of *A Farewell to Arms,* he had, over the last ten years, written many of his best stories and articles in all of America's major publications, published *To Have and Have Not,* and contributed much correspondence from the war in Spain. People who had not read Hemingway were introduced to him through the 1932 film version of *A Farewell to Arms* with Gary Cooper. With his exploits in Europe and Africa now well known, the author was the epitome of American adventurism and (whether he liked it or not) an international celebrity. In short, he was the perfect candidate to lure Hollywood's elite and wealthy adventure seekers to Sun Valley.

The Sun Valley honeymoon didn't last long. One of the men who had convinced Hemingway to accept the resort's offer, Gene van Guilder, was killed in a shooting accident. Hemingway was asked to speak at the funeral. Hemingway had not known van Guilder for long but his eulogy was poignant and heartfelt, so much so that the words he spoke would adorn Hemingway's own tombstone 22 years later:

Best of all he loved the fall
The leaves yellow on the cottonwoods
Leaves floating on the trout streams and above the hills
The high blue windless skies
… Now he will be a part of them forever

Hoping to rendezvous with his sons for Christmas, Hemingway headed to Key West only to find the house empty. As she had promised, Pauline had left with the boys before he arrived. Their divorce was granted on terms of abandonment, and Pauline was given full custody of their sons.

For Whom the Bell Tolls was released in October 1940. Hemingway married Martha Gellhorn at the Union Pacific Railroad dining room in Cheyenne,

Wyoming, in December 1940. When Martha and her friends Lloyd and Tillie Arnold read the new novel, they suspected that Hemingway's father had killed himself. After confirming their assumption, Hemingway spoke of his "common sense view of suicide" and calmly explained to his new wife how he would go about it, with a shotgun, using a toe to pull the trigger.[2] Hemingway was forced to think about death when F. Scott Fitzgerald died that December, and Max Perkins, Hemingway's friend and editor at Scribner's since 1924, died in 1941. Pauline Hemingway died in 1951.

Hemingway's marriage to Martha Gellhorn ended in 1945, and he married journalist Mary Welsh in 1946. He never returned to the Clark's Fork Valley or Cooke City but this "good country" stayed in his heart and in his work. In *Across the River and into the Trees,* Colonel Cantwell hails from Montana and at one point argues that Cooke City is the toughest town in the world. In *Islands in the Stream*, protagonist Thomas Hudson also hails from Montana, and he implores his writer friend to head to his ranch for inspiration. The Tom character would reappear in "A Man of the World," published in the centennial anniversary edition of *The Atlantic Monthly* in 1957. This was the last story Hemingway published in his lifetime and it was set in Cooke City. In *True at First Light,* published after his death, he would refer to the General Store in Cooke City, from where he had mailed so much of his work to Max Perkins during the thirties.

Even in his later years after much deterioration and electric shock therapy, Hemingway's heart remained in the Yellowstone High Country. In 1961, less than a month before his death, Charles Scribner sent Hemingway a copy of a fly fishing guide to Yellowstone. Carlos Baker wrote that the book "set him dreaming of the old days at the Nordquist ranch beside the Clark's Fork of the Yellowstone."[3] A few days before committing suicide, Hemingway called his old friend Chub Weaver. After all those nights around the campfire and their rides over the Beartooth Mountains thirty years earlier, Weaver was not surprised at the way his friend chose to end his life.[4]

Ernest Hemingway first entered the Yellowstone High Country in the summer of 1930. He left for the last time in the fall of 1939. He was at his best over those years, as a hunter, as a fisherman, as a family man, but most of all, as a writer.

*He could feel his heart beat against the pine needle floor of the forest.**

*The final line from *For Whom the Bell Tolls.*

Conclusion

Why is there seemingly unending interest in Ernest Hemingway? Is there any other author with such a recognizable image? If you were to walk up to anyone in the street and show them a picture of Hemingway, how many would recognize him? How many people could recognize Steinbeck or Fitzgerald? Why are there new biographies and movies about his life? There are even posthumous releases of his work almost sixty years after his death, and new interpretations of his known work still being offered. What is it about this author that generates such sustained interest bordering on obsession? In the words of my friend Dink Bruce, there is simply no end to this shit. Why?

First, think about when he lived. Hemingway was born in 1899 and died in 1961. He was born at a time when people lived without electricity, phones, and cars, and died in the age of space travel, television, and nuclear energy. The changes that took place during his lifetime were immense. Second, consider the life he chose to live: married four times, father of three children, a volunteer in WWI, resident of Paris during the Roaring Twenties, traveler of Europe, Africa, and the Caribbean, and eyewitness to the Spanish Civil War and WWII. He grew up idolizing Theodore Roosevelt and wrote one of his final letters to John F. Kennedy.

Next, consider the life he didn't choose: one of five children, dressed as a girl by his mother until he was seven, and immersed in a culture of hunting and fishing by his father in an effort to compensate. He lived through the suicide of his father, the Great Depression, and the rise of fascism and communism.

He was a father, son, husband, brother, friend, enemy, soldier (sort of), writer, journalist, adventurer, alcoholic, and eventually, a suicide. In short, he was a fascinating individual who lived during an important time in human history. While it is important not to be an apologist for Hemingway as he was a deeply flawed individual, at the same time it is important to understand the life he led in order to fully appreciate his work.

Finally, examine his profession and how he chose to go about it. He was a writer and he was prolific. He wrote fifty-seven short stories, seven novels, a Pulitzer Prize-winning novella, two works of non-fiction presented as novels, a play, numerous dispatches, essays, and columns, and a wealth of work that has been released posthumously. Hemingway wrote so many letters that it will take seventeen volumes to document them all. In his fiction he used a technique that has become cliché in the world of Hemingway criticism. In an interview with George Plimpton in the *Paris Review*, Hemingway explained the iceberg theory. "If it is any use to know it, I always try to write on the principle of the iceberg. There is seven eighths of it underwater for every part that shows." The words represent the tip of the iceberg; the meaning behind the words is the mass that lies beneath. It is up to the reader to decipher that meaning. The vast majority of his work is autobiographical to some extent. This means that one may read a story once and grasp the tip of the iceberg. The same reader may then examine the story more closely and discover the meaning that lies below the surface. Next, knowing Hemingway's biography, the reader may recognize the story as reflecting a certain time in the author's life, and then read the story in a different way.

In the world of Hemingway criticism there is one school that demands the work be separated from the biography, and that each work must be assessed on its own merits without other context. I am of the school that believes his biography is essential to fully understanding his work.

Hemingway's intentional use of ambiguity allows a reader to pull different meanings from the work as the reader's own life changes. One may read a story as a young man and pull certain meaning from it, and then return as an older man and find completely different meaning. When all of these different factors and variables are combined, the result is a literary mystery, both historical and personal, that can take a lifetime to unravel.

Until now, Hemingway's connection to the Yellowstone High Country had somehow remained vague. His time here had been touched on by biographers, but considering how other aspects of his life, work, and psyche have been exhaustively dissected, one wonders why this important part of his life wasn't examined as thoroughly. In order to fully unravel the mystery that is Hemingway, we have to fully understand the years he spent in this remote wilderness. To understand the bitterness and resentment Harry shows to his wife in "The Snows of Kilimanjaro," we have to consider Hemingway's 1930 stay at St. Vincent's Hospital with Pauline at his side. When we assess Robert Jordan's struggles with his father's suicide in *For Whom the Bell Tolls,* we have to do so with the knowledge that Hemingway used his experiences in these mountains as a salve to ease the pain of his own father's suicide. When we read Hemingway's final story and cringe at the violence at the center of it, we must familiarize ourselves with the culture of violence prevalent around Cooke City during Hemingway's time here.

This endeavor, which began when my old friend "Walkin'" Tom Weaver came into my coffee shop with that copy of *True at First Light,* has taken me many places. I sat with Patrick Hemingway at a bar in Bozeman talking about Tom's father "Chub" and his friendship with Patrick's father. I went to the Firestone Library at Princeton University and donned the "white gloves" as I carefully picked through the photographs of the Patrick Hemingway Collection.

In the summer of 2018 I found myself at the International Hemingway Conference in Paris. I was there to present a paper connecting Hemingway's final story to my hometown and to support a joint proposal to bring the next conference to the communities of Sheridan, Wyoming, and Cooke City, Montana. In a surreal moment at the Eiffel Tower on the first morning of the conference, I was pulled into the foyer by the president of the Hemingway Society and told that our proposal had won and that the next conference would indeed be in Yellowstone Country. The following day the announcement was made public in The Richelieu Amphitheater at the Sorbonne.

In a few short years, I had gone from making lattes in Cooke City to hosting the 2020 International Hemingway Conference. I will be forever grateful to all the people who helped and encouraged me along the way, to the world of Hemingway scholarship that has taken my research seriously, and to Hemingway himself, whose life and work have taken me on the literary adventure of a lifetime.

APPENDIX I

Hemingway's Work in the Yellowstone High Country

1928

After the birth of his second son Ernest Hemingway headed west for the first time in order to finish his then untitled novel. It was his first time in the Rocky Mountains and while he didn't quite make it to Yellowstone Country, he did make it as far as Sheridan, Wyoming, and the surrounding Bighorn Mountains. He began his work that summer at the Folly Ranch in the Bighorns, then headed back into town, working for four days at the Sheridan Inn before returning to the mountains to finish what would become *A Farewell to Arms* at the Spear-O-Wigwam Ranch. The Bighorn Mountains are not in the Yellowstone area, but Hemingway's work there did establish a routine of heading to the western mountains in order to finish projects.

1930

Upon arriving at the L—T Ranch for the first time, Hemingway went to work arranging his Nick Adams stories for the re-issue of *In Our Time*. He also tried to address what Max Perkins considered libelous parts of some of the stories, eventually deciding to leave the stories as they were regardless of the legal risk. After the laborious work on the short story collection, Hemingway worked on *Death in the Afternoon*. In letters to Max Perkins, his editor at Scribner's, he says he was writing six days a week and had written 40,000 words, and he was in possession of "six more cases of beer" which he believed would get him through six more chapters.

1932

Hemingway wrote the short story "The Light of the World" in early August at the L—T. He then re-edited and approved the final proofs of *Death in the Afternoon* and mailed off his final draft from the Cooke City General Store. Apart from that, most of the work he did that summer was trying to sell short stories he had already written to the highest bidder and writing letters to critics and friends.

1936

This summer Hemingway worked furiously on *To Have and Have Not*. Even with the Spanish Civil War starting, he was determined to finish his novel before going to Spain to cover the conflict, perhaps thinking that the war might consume his life and work for a long time. On September 26 he wrote to his editor that he had written more than 55,000 words and was going to finish the first draft by October.

1938

This trip to the L—T Ranch was particularly busy for Hemingway. His first work was to order the stories for *The First Forty-nine Stories*, write the book's preface, and send everything off to his editor for immediate publication. With this task completed, he went to work on his Spanish Civil War stories. In a letter to Arnold Gingrich he described "Night Before Battle" as some of the best work he had done, and author John Steinbeck considered "The Butterfly and the Tank" one of the finest short stories of all time. The third story he worked on was "The Denunciation." All three stories appeared in Gingrich's *Esquire* magazine over the next few months. In the same letter to Gingrich, Hemingway mentioned writing the first two chapters of his latest novel, signifying the beginning of *For Whom the Bell Tolls*.

1939

In February 1939 *Vogue* published "The Clark's Fork Valley, Wyoming," Hemingway's synopsis of his time at the L—T. It is unclear when or where he actually wrote it but it was most likely taken from notes made at the ranch over the years. The memories were very personal. Later that summer he continued to work on *For Whom the Bell Tolls.* Before heading to the mountains that year, he mentioned in several letters that he was struggling with the novel's snowstorm scene and was going to the mountains for inspiration, so he may have written the scene at the ranch. Another scene that Hemingway may have written at the ranch was based on the time Hemingway and Chub Weaver rode horses over Beartooth Pass and Hemingway dropped the gun that his father had used to kill himself into Froze-to-Death Lake.

The Yellowstone High Country in the Work

The Yellowstone High Country appears in the following twelve works by Ernest Hemingway:

Novels
For Whom the Bell Tolls
Across the River and into the Trees
Islands in the Steam

Non-fiction in novel form
Green Hills of Africa
True at First Light.

Short stories
"Wine of Wyoming"
"The Gambler, the Nun, and the Radio"
"Father's and Sons"
"The Snows of Kilimanjaro"
"A Man of the World"

Essays
"Clark's Fork Valley, Wyoming"
Preface to *The First Forty-nine Stories*

While the L—T is not mentioned by name, it is referred to as "the ranch" in many of these works. Cooke City is named in the three novels and the collection of stories. In some cases, these references are long and descriptive; in others they are brief and oblique. Three of the stories and one of the essays are set entirely in the region. All of these instances are important when studied individually; when considered together, they demonstrate the significant influence the Yellowstone High Country had on Hemingway.

Winner Take Nothing 1933

The final three stories in this collection represent Hemingway's first three visits to the Rockies.

"Wine of Wyoming"

This story takes place in Sheridan, Wyoming, in 1928. That summer Hemingway stayed at the Folly Ranch, the Spear-O-Wigwam Ranch, and the Sheridan Inn. Hemingway was finishing *A Farewell to Arms* this summer. While staying at the Sheridan Inn, Hemingway ventured into downtown Sheridan and struck up a friendship with a French family called the Moncinis, who worked at the nearby mine and lived on Val Vista Street. Much of the story is in French and revolves around bootlegging. Hemingway and his wife spoke French and the Moncinis made wine and beer, which made for an easy relationship between the two couples.

"The Gambler, the Nun, and the Radio"

Published in 1933, this story takes place entirely in an unnamed hospital in a town called Hailey, Montana. It is based on Hemingway's six-week convalescence at St Vincent's Hospital in Billings in late 1930. After an eventful summer and fall at the L—T Ranch, Hemingway, fellow author John Dos Passos,

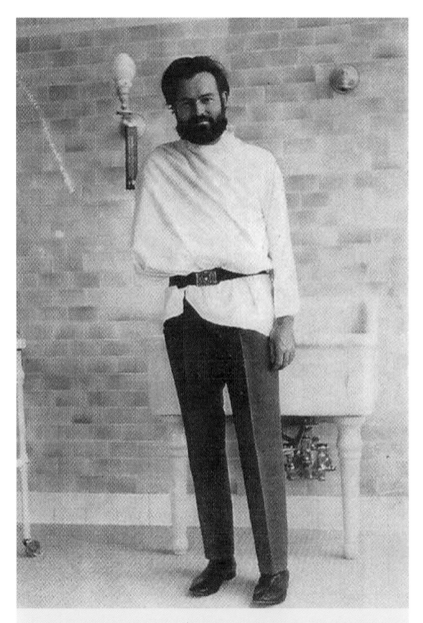

A bandaged Hemingway poses in St. Vincent's Hospital in Billings, Montana, in 1930. His long stay there inspired his short story, "The Gambler, the Nun, and the Radio."

PHOTO PROVIDED BY THE AUTHOR.

and local guide Floyd Allington set out for Key West in Hemingway's Model A Ford that had carried him through bullfight seasons in Spain. They went though Cooke City, then through the northern end of Yellowstone, staying at Mammoth Hot Springs. Near Laurel, Montana, they drove off the road and wrecked.

Hemingway suffered an oblique spiral fracture to his writing arm, a serious injury. He stayed at the hospital for six weeks, undergoing many complications that left Hemingway in a foul mood for most of his stay. The story doesn't convey that mood and is fairly light-hearted. The gambler in the title is a Mexican named "Cayetano" who has been shot twice in the stomach over a card game. He earns the writer's admiration with the way he handles his injury. Hemingway always felt that injury and misfortune, both physical and emotional, were inevitable in every man's life. The way each man handled these inevitabilities was what defined him. Cayetano is a perfect example of this: he is resilient and stoic while his Russian counterpart and fellow patient screams and complains about his less serious injury.

"Fathers and Sons"

Nick Adams, the literary embodiment of Hemingway as a child and young man and the protagonist in many of Hemingway's earlier stories, re-emerges in this story as an adult with a son. Nick fondly remembers his father and assesses the things he did well (teaching Nick to hunt and fish) and the things he did not do well (teach him about sex). This is the first time since his father's suicide that Hemingway discusses his father in his fiction. While driving with his son, who is based on Bumby, the son asks why they never go to visit his grandfather's grave. The boy then considers the death of Nick, his own father: "I hope we won't live somewhere so that I can never go to pray at your tomb when you are dead." After promising to arrange it, Adams and his son try to figure out a convenient place to intern the family and they settle on "the ranch." "Couldn't we all be buried out at the ranch?" This exchange at the end of "Fathers and Sons" demonstrates Hemingway's long struggle with his father's death and the healing quality provided by the L—T.

Green Hills of Africa
1935

Green Hills of Africa is a non-fiction account of Hemingway's first trip to Africa in 1933. Hemingway was accompanied by his wife Pauline and Charles Thompson, both of whom hunted with Hemingway in the Yellowstone High Country the previous year. This is very much a hunting book, and since all three participants had hunted the country around the ranch, there are inevitable comparisons between the two places.

At one point, Hemingway explains a strategy used by his favorite African guide to harvest the liver and kidneys of a reedbuck while still managing to carry out the whole animal. Droopy, the guide, would gut the buck and then wrap the liver and kidneys in the stomach and tie it to the end of a stick, enabling him to carry it over his shoulder like a hobo: "It was a good trick and I thought how I would show it to John Staib in Wyoming some time and he would smile his deaf man's smile (you had to throw a pebble at him to make him stop when you heard a bull bugle), and I knew what John would say. He would say, 'By Godd, Urnust, dot's smardt.'" John Staebe (correct spelling) homesteaded the Ghost Creek Ranch in Crandall, Wyoming; he hunted with Hemingway several times in the thirties. The mention of Staebe in *Green Hills of Africa* again points to Hemingway's admiration of people who handle their injuries stoically.

Another time in the book Hemingway sees a comparison to hunting deer in Wyoming: "I've hunted a country just like this for deer. The south slope of Timber Creek in Wyoming." A few pages later: "I do not smoke, and hunting at home I have several times smelled elk in the rutting season before I have seen them and I can smell clearly where an old bull has lain in the forest. The bull elk has a strong musky smell. It is a strong but pleasant odor and I know it well." This quote is interesting for several reasons. First, it dispels the myth that Hemingway was a smoker; while he might have smoked occasionally as a young man (see "The Big Two-Hearted River") or perhaps indulged in a cigar while fishing with Castro, he generally did not smoke and absolutely didn't smoke while hunting, since it would affect his sense of smell and possibly reveal his presence to wary game. More importantly, in this quote, he refers to the Yellowstone High Country as "home."

Hunting elk is also referenced later: "…he was no more like a real bull than a spike elk is like a big, old, thick-necked, dark-maned, wonder-horned, tawny-hided, beer-horse-built bugler of a bull-elk."

Green Hills of Africa gives the fullest account of the injury Hemingway sustained during the 1930 car accident, and some insight into how it changed him as a hunter. Hemingway describes watching flies torment a horse under its tail; he sympathizes with the horse and then explains that one thing that gave him more horror was his recuperation in the Billings hospital after breaking his arm. After giving a graphic depiction of the injury and the complicated recovery, he compares his situation with that of a wounded elk:

> "Alone with the pain in the night in the fifth week of not sleeping I thought suddenly how a bull elk must feel if you break a shoulder and he gets away and in that night I lay and felt it all, the whole thing as it would happen from the shock of the bullet to the end of the business and, being a little out of my head, thought perhaps what I was going through was a punishment for all hunters."

The slightly delirious author then rationalizes his predicament and vows to become a better hunter as a result of his misfortune:

> "I had been shot and I had been crippled and gotten away. I expected, always, to be killed by one thing or another and I, truly, did not mind that any more. Since I still loved to hunt I resolved that I would only shoot as long I could kill cleanly and as soon as I lost that ability I would stop."

In this book he compares the game, the guides, and the terrain of East Africa to that of the Clark's Fork Valley, specifically Timber Creek at the headwaters of Crandall Creek. Even on another continent with plenty to occupy him, Hemingway's thoughts drifted back to the Yellowstone High Country.

"The Snows of Kilimanjaro"
1936

"The Snows of Kilimanjaro" is one of Hemingway's best and most famous stories.

In it, the autobiographic Harry lies dying in sight of the great African mountain. The story is told in two parts. While Harry is conscious, he is inexplicably cruel to his wife Helen, who tends to his wounds, gives him food and drink, and even shoots an antelope for them to eat as they await rescue. The other part of the story involves hallucinations, dreams, or memories that overcome Harry as he loses consciousness. Hemingway would later claim that the hallucinatory parts of the story could have comprised four novels.

Harry is resentful toward Helen partly because of her wealth. Pauline, Hemingway's wife at the time, was very wealthy. Her uncle Gus had funded the African safari that inspired the story. After the 1930 car accident that landed Hemingway in St. Vincent's Hospital in Billings, Pauline tended to her husband for more than a month. He was worried about losing the use of his right arm, the one he used for writing, shooting, and fishing. There were medical setbacks and multiple surgeries and a steady stream of morphine and bootleg liquor. When his friend Archie MacLeish arrived to check on him, Hemingway accused his visitor of coming to watch him die. This poisonous, paranoid episode provides insight into what sort of abuse Pauline may have suffered at the hands of her ailing husband, and by the end of Hemingway's convalescence, many of their friends felt more sorry for Pauline than for her husband. These incidents suggest that Hemingway's stay in the hospital may have inspired the dialogue between Harry and Helen in "The Snows of Kilimanjaro."

This story also contains a direct reference to the Yellowstone High Country and to Clark's Fork Valley folklore. In one of the hallucinatory flashbacks toward the end of the piece, Harry laments all the stories he had yet to write. It is not the unwritten stories of Paris that haunt the dying writer, it is the stories of the Yellowstone High Country and his time at the ranch:

No, had never written about Paris. Not the Paris that he cared about. But what about the rest that he had never written?

> What about the ranch and the silvered gray of the sage-brush, the quick clear water in the irrigation ditches, and the heavy green of the alfalfa. The trail went up into the hills and the cattle in the summer were shy as deer. The bawling and the steady noise and slow moving mass raising a dust as you brought them down in the fall. And behind the mountains, the clear sharpness of the peak in the evening light and, riding down along the trail in the moonlight, bright across the valley. Now he remembered coming down through the timber in the dark holding the horse's tail when you could not see and all the stories that he meant to write.

From here Harry tells the story of the 1912 murder of Jim Smith. Smith was the original homesteader of what later became the L—T Ranch. He later moved up the valley to what is now the RDS Ranch. During the winter of 1912, the owner of the L—T, a man named Kitchen, left young Tony Rodoscheck in charge of the ranch and instructed him not to loan out any hay. As Kitchen headed out on snowshoes toward Cooke City, he stopped at the RDS and sold some hay to Smith. In the spring, when Smith headed to the L—T to get his hay, he was confronted by Rodoscheck. The two already had a little history: Rodoscheck had worked for Smith (by all accounts an ornery cuss) and had been run off his ranch, unpaid, with a beating. As Smith made his move for the hay, Rodoscheck shot him in the elbow.

Smith fell out of the hayloft and bled out under a tree. Smith's body was hauled out on horseback and Tony Rodoscheck was exonerated on the grounds of justifiable homicide, as was the custom in those days. Hemingway inserts Harry into the story and has him ski the body and the killer down to Cody to face justice. In this way Smith has been immortalized in "The Snows of Kilimajaro." Today, Jim Smith Peak towers over the upper Clark's Fork Valley.

The Fifth Column and The First Forty-nine Stories
1938

In this work, Hemingway offers four new stories, his previously unpublished first story, and the forty-four stories already published in his first three collections, as well as his only attempt at playwriting. The preface to this mammoth undertaking was written at the L—T Ranch. In it, he discusses his favorite places to write, starting with Madrid: "It was always a good place for working. So was Paris, and so were Key West, Florida, in the cool months and the ranch, near Cooke City, Montana." This is the first time Cooke City was mentioned in print by Hemingway, and he placed it on a list of his favorite places to write in the world.

"Clark's Fork Valley, Wyoming"
1939

This essay was written in 1939 for *Vogue* magazine. It begins with a casual description of the habits of trout in the Clark's Fork around September, but as the piece progresses it becomes a deeply personal account of Hemingway's time in the Yellowstone High Country. His remembrances span all the years he spent at the ranch. There is the fishing, the grizzlies up Timber Creek, the heaving chests of giant bull elk in the rut, and the old bighorn sheep on the slopes of Pilot and Index peaks. There are memories of his sons learning to fish and ride horses. The piece is short and Hemingway chooses his words carefully, picks a few of his most memorable experiences, and describes them in concise detail to represent his time there as a whole.

When *Vogue* commissioned him for an article, this essay was probably not what the *Vogue* editors were expecting. They had caught the writer between his final two visits to the ranch, after the fall of Spain, after the construction of the Beartooth Highway, with his marriage damaged beyond repair, and his time in the Yellowstone High Country coming to a close. While *Vogue* was likely hoping for a travel piece on the wonderfulness of Hemingway's western home, it got a eulogy on Hemingway's time in one of his very favorite places. It is packed with bittersweet remembrance, and there is no looking to the future. Hemingway writes the entire essay in the past tense, until the final line.

The essay starts with words, "At the end of summer...." The second paragraph begins, "The nights were cold...." The first page ends with, "the sage was silvery grey." From here Hemingway drifts into dreamy reminiscence of all the good times at the ranch. This reminiscence is deeply personal. Three of the last four paragraphs start with the words "You remembered" as if he were writing to himself. In the final paragraph Hemingway uses physical imagery and landscape to close the door on this chapter of his life: "Then there was the winter; the trees bare now, the snow blowing so you could not see, the saddle wet, then frozen as you came downhill....It's a good country." The author switches to the present tense in the final line in order to preserve the landscape; his assessment of the "good country" is declarative and permanent.

This piece appeared in the February issue of *Vogue* and then largely disappeared until popping up 28 years later in *By-line: Ernest Hemingway* in 1967 and then 33 years after that in *Hemingway on Fishing*, published in 2000. William Kittredge, who taught creative writing at the University of Montana, recognized the importance of this piece when he chose to include it in his anthology, *The Portable Western Reader*. Of all of Hemingway's work, Kittredge chose this little piece because it "clearly shows Hemingway's style and the reasons he chose to weather the closing seasons of his life in the West." For the first time, instead of being grouped with contemporaries such as Fitzgerald and Stein, Kittredge places Hemingway alongside writers of the American West such as Steinbeck, Jeffers, and Norman Maclean, perhaps more fitting company considering Hemingway's love of the West during the second half of his life.

For Whom the Bell Tolls
1940

While the novel is set in the mountains of Spain, the main character, partly autobiographical and partly fictional, is from Red Lodge, Montana. In shaping Robert Jordan, Hemingway uses Major Robert Merriman, an American fighting with the Spanish Loyalists, some of his own biography, some of his friend Chub Weaver's biography, and a collage of experiences from his time in the Yellowstone High Country to lend depth to the character, give him a home, and explain his prowess with guns, horses, and mountain travel. Jordan is a Spanish professor at the University of Montana, explaining his fluency in the language.

Much of the natural description in *For Whom the Bell Tolls* can be traced directly to the Yellowstone High Country. In chapter 14, for example, as the snowstorm moves in, Jordan remembers encountering a moose in similar conditions back home in Montana: "In a snowstorm you rode up to a moose and he mistook your horse for another moose and trotted forward to meet you. In a snowstorm it always seemed, for a time, as there were no enemies." This encounter with a moose happened to Hemingway in 1932 as he rode down Timber Creek alone to check the early reviews of *Death in the Afternoon.*

As the novel nears its end, Jordan flashes back more and more to his home in the mountains. In chapter 37, after comparing Maria's hair to that of marten when released from a trap, he compares the band of Spanish Loyalists to his friends in America: "Anselmo is my oldest friend. I know him better than I know Charles, than I know Chub, than I know Guy, than I know Mike, and I know them well." While Anselmo was a fictional character, the rest of the men mentioned were Hemingway's best friends at that time: Charles Thompson, Guy Hickock, Henry "Mike" Strater, and Leland "Chub" Weaver.

For Whom the Bell Tolls is the novel in which Hemingway deals with his relationship with his father. In addition to the early Nick Adams stories, Hemingway had touched on the subject rather poignantly in "Fathers and Sons" and mentioned his father's suicide in "Homage to Switzerland," but Hemingway had not properly addressed his complex adult feelings toward his father until this novel. Hemingway's mother had dressed him as a girl until he was six or seven years old, and his father, in an attempt to reverse this trend, had taken young Ernest into the woods every summer to show him how to hunt and fish. On page 338 of the first edition, Hemingway confronts his conflicted feelings about his father through the character Robert Jordan: "I'll never forget how sick it made me the first time I knew he was a cobarde. Go on, say it in English. Coward." Through Jordan, Hemingway calls his father a coward not just because of the suicide in particular, but because of the general situation that led to it. In the same passage Jordan says, "He wasn't any son of a bitch, though. He was just a coward and that was the worst luck any man could have. Because if he wasn't a coward he would have stood up to that woman and not let her bully him." Here Hemingway confronts what he considered his father's greatest failure, and then has Robert Jordan speculate on how his life may have been different if his father had married someone else.

In Chapter 41, Jordan recalls saying goodbye to his father while leaving home for the first time. For Jordan, this takes place as he is boarding the train in Red Lodge, Montana, to leave for college. For Hemingway, one imagines this taking place as he left Oak Park, Michigan, for WWI as an eighteen-year-old. Jordan recalls, "he had taken the train at Red Lodge to go down to Billings to get the train there to go away to school for the first time. He had been afraid to go and he did not want any one to know it…." As his father kisses Jordan goodbye and offers a biblical quotation to convey the emotion of the moment, Hemingway addresses the moment when children finally see their parents as the real but flawed people they are: "But his mustache had been moist and his eyes were damp with emotion and Robert Jordan had been so embarrassed by all of it, the damp religious sound of the prayer, and by his father kissing him good-by, that he had felt suddenly so much older than his father and sorry for him that he could hardly bear it." As the train pulls out of the station, Jordan stands on the rear platform of the train watching the water tower at the station grow smaller and smaller until the point that both the station and the water tower are "now minute and tiny in the steady clicking that was taking him away." The water tower is an obvious metaphor for his father and the station represents his home. With the diminishing of his father and the departure from his home, Jordan enters manhood.

Clarence Hemingway had committed suicide just before his son's first trip out West. This traumatic event pre-occupied the writer throughout his time here, and he had carried the gun his father had used to shoot himself with him during his time in the mountains. Around guns and death all the time in the Clark's Fork Valley, Hemingway discussed suicide with friends at the ranch and with other friends and family through letters. When trying to channel courage from his grandfather, Robert Jordan laments, "Maybe he sent me what little I have through that other one that misused the gun."

In Chapter 30 there is a detailed account of Jordan dropping the gun that killed his father into a lake in the Beartooth Mountains:

> ...he had ridden up to the top of the high country above Red Lodge, with Chub, where they had built the road to Cooke City now over the pass and across the Bear Tooth Plateau, and up there where the wind was thin and there was snow all summer on the hills they had stopped by the lake which was supposed to be eight hundred feet deep and was a deep green color, and Chub held the two horses and he climbed out on a rock and leaned over and saw his face in the still water, and saw himself holding the gun, and then he dropped it, holding it by the muzzle, and saw it go down making bubbles until it was just as big as a watch charm in that clear water, and then it was out of sight. Then he came back off the rock and when he swung up into the saddle he gave old Bess such a clout with the spurs she started to buck like an old rocking horse. He bucked her out along the shore of the lake and as soon as she was reasonable they went back along the trail.
> "I know why you did that with the old gun, Bob," Chub said.
> "Well, then we don't have to talk about it," he had said.

The episode with the gun happened in real life just as it was described in the novel. According to Chub's son Tom Weaver, who lived in Red Lodge until his death in 2017, the lake in question was Froze-to-Death Lake on the Beartooth Plateau.

As *For Whom the Bell Tolls* comes to its conclusion, we see more and more references to the author's decade in the Yellowstone High Country. As Jordan ties the explosives to the bridge he takes time to look down at the stream be-neath him, "As he looked a trout rose for some insect and made a circle on the surface…." The horse that whisks Maria to safety is white faced much like Old Bess, Ernest's favorite horse at the ranch. Robert Jordan's broken bone can be seen pushing up the flesh up much like Hemingway's broken arm in 1930. As Jordan lies dying, waiting to shoot the officer pursuing his comrades, he has one more thought about his father: "I don't want to do that business my father did." Then, trying to keep himself from losing consciousness, he tells himself "Think about Montana." And finally, the last line of the book: "He could feel his heart beating against the pine needle floor of the forest."

Across the River and into the Trees
1950

Published in 1950, *Across the River and into the Trees* was Hemingway's fifth novel. It is the story of an ailing American colonel, Richard Cantwell, and his affair with Renata, a young Italian countess. Most of action takes place in Venice, but the book begins with a duck hunt on a frozen pond, after which, Cantwell is driven through the countryside by his driver "Jackson," who is from Rawlins, Wyoming. Because Cantwell is from Montana and Jackson is from Wyoming, the two discuss towns, landmarks, and legends from the two states periodically throughout the book.

Toward the end of Chapter 5, as they approach Venice, the two men talk about the toughest towns they know. Cantwell suggests that Venice is about as tough as it gets. After Casper and Cheyenne, both in Wyoming, are discussed briefly, Cantwell declares: "O.K., Jackson. Maybe we move in different circles. Or maybe we have a differing definition for the word. But this town of Venice, with everybody being polite and having good manners, is as tough as Cooke City, Montana, on the day they have the Old Timers' Fish Fry." Cooke City is indeed a tough town, and the Old Timers' Fish Fry was a tradition in Heming-way's day. There is a picture of the 1930 Fish Fry above the piano in Hoosiers Bar in Cooke City.

In Chapter 29, Cantwell declares that he was in the Montana National Guard as a sixteen-year-old. If this mean he was from Montana, it would make him the third Hemingway protagonist from the state, joining Robert Jordan of *For Whom the Bell Tolls* and Thomas Hudson from *Islands in the Stream.*

In Chapter 37, as the book draws to a close, Cantwell plans a trip to Wyoming for him and his young lover. After describing the pines and cottonwoods, and the yellowing of aspen in the fall, he returns to his 1928 trip to Sheridan and the surrounding mountains to plot their imaginary itinerary: "Sheridan lays right up against them. There aren't any foothills to the Bighorns. They rise high out of the plateau. You can see Clouds Peak."

He suggests they head toward Billings, stopping to see the site of the Wagon Box Fight and the Battle of Little Big Horn "where they killed that fool George Armstrong Custer."

"A Man of the World" 1957

This strange, savage little story is set in fictitious Jessup. The inspiration for this setting is quite obviously Cooke City, Montana.

During Hemingway's first two trips to the Yellowstone High Country in 1930 and 1932, Prohibition was still the law of the land, but when he returned in 1936 Prohibition was over and there were bars in Cooke City. Grace Anderson, who worked at Hoosiers Bar and Motel in the 1930s, remembered Hemingway coming in mornings or afternoons. The bar was open 24 hours a day. "We never closed," she said. "He'd sit at the end of the bar and push his glass across the bar when he wanted another drink. He was not one to visit; we had the impression he was there to write his books and didn't want to bother with anyone." This quote is important because it puts Ernest Hemingway at Hoosiers Bar in Cooke City. It is also important because it sheds some light on where he found his inspiration for "A Man of the World." In the story, Hemingway writes, "Then The Index was open all night long and got the early morning trade and from daylight until ten o'clock in the morning the drinks

In an essay about his time in the Clark's Fork Valley, Hemingway wrote, "Up the river were the two peaks of Pilot and Index." This photo shows the prominent peaks that Hemingway saw from the L—T Ranch, Pilot on the left and Index on the right. The names of the peaks became the names of the two bars in "A Man of the World," the last short story Hemingway published in his lifetime.
PATRICK HEMINGWAY PAPERS, C0066, MANUSCRIPTS DIVISION, DEPARTMENT OF RARE BOOKS AND SPECIAL COLLECTIONS, PRINCETON UNIVERSITY LIBRARY.

were on the house....they did not have to do that kind of thing. But that was the way they were.

The two bars in "A Man of the World" are called "The Pilot" and "The Index." Pilot and Index are two prominent mountains that Hemingway looked at every morning at the ranch. They sit about three miles from Cooke City, and when approaching from the east they dominate the landscape for about fifteen miles. There are still only two bars in Cooke City, and Hoosiers is still one of them. The bar altercation around which the story revolves will resonate with anyone who has been to Cooke City in the winter: "They were fighting on the ice of the road with the snow all banked up and the light from this door and the Index door."

The story is short, barely three pages, but there are other lines that describe Cooke City, both now and in the 1930s. About the two watering holes: "... they were both good saloons with old-days bars..." The complicated layout of town: "'What do you mean those roads? Somebody asked him. 'you only go on one road.'" The weather: "On this night it was really cold outside and he came in with icicles on his mustache...." The nightlife: "At the poker game there were just gamblers sitting there and cutting each other up. It was a quiet evening on a weeknight in town and there wasn't any excitement. The place wasn't making a nickel except at the bar."

On the first page of "A Man of the World," Hemingway mentions Pilot and Index seven times, Cooke City is the only town within 60 miles of Pilot and Index; it is a town with one road and a couple of good saloons with old-days bars. It is a town that gets unbearably cold, and the snow banks up, and you can still find people playing gambling machines and an occasional poker game. It is also a town Hemingway frequented during the thirties, visiting bars in "the mornings or afternoons." You would not meet tourists at Hoosiers bar in the mornings, you would meet the old-timers, like the ones he met on the trails of the Clark's Fork Valley, or the old-timers he mentions that buy a few bullets from the Cooke City General Store in *True at First Light*, the kind of old-timers that might tell a story one morning at the bar about the rough and tumble old days, when the mine went bust and everyone left, then one night there was this terrible fight out front of the bar....

The fight in "A Man of the World" is particularly gruesome, almost to the point of being unbelievable, but many of the stories Hemingway would have heard during his time in the mountains were just as gruesome. Jack Crandall, the man that Crandall Creek was named after, was prospecting with his partner along the creek. They were found beheaded with their heads mounted on their pickaxes. The murders were blamed on the Crow Indians but it was widely believed that rival prospectors were the culprits. In 1912 the original owner of the B-4 ranch, Jim Smith, was shot to death by a ranch hand, an event mentioned by Hemingway in "The Snows of Kilimanjaro." In 1931 Budd Hart, a local stonemason who had done much of the stonework at the ranches, was involved in an altercation with two men at a Cooke City bar. Shots were exchanged, and the two other men involved, Les Lightner and Walt Mcall, decided to go to Hart's cabin to settle things. Hart was lying in wait, killed the two men, cut up their bodies with an axe, and stashed the pieces in the woodshed. Hart hoped everything would blow over by spring, but he was found out, arrested, and tried. But just as in the death of Jim Smith, the verdict was justifiable homicide. The Budd Hart killings happened in 1931 between Hemingway's first and second visits to the area, so he would have been well aware of the way things went down in that part of the world at that time. After hearing these stories, the fight in "A Man of the World" doesn't sound quite so shocking.

After the five stories of the Spanish Civil War were published in 1938 and 1939, Hemingway published only four more short stories in his lifetime: "The Good Lion" and "The Faithful Bull," both children's stories published in 1951, and "Get a Seeing-Eyed Dog" and "A Man of the World" published as "Two Tales of Darkness" in the 100th anniversary edition of *The Atlantic Monthly* in 1957. These were the last things Hemingway published in his lifetime. According to Carlos Baker's biography of Hemingway, "Get a Seeing-Eyed Dog" was written in 1956 while "A Man of the World" was written in 1957. This makes "A Man of the World," set in Cooke City, Montana, the final published work of Hemingway's life.

Islands in the Stream
1970

Islands in the Stream was published posthumously in 1970. The story takes place between 1938 and the end of WWII. It is presented in three parts: the first in Bimini, the second in Cuba, and the third aboard a boat in the Caribbean.

Six pages into the novel, as the reader is introduced to Thomas Hudson, one of Hemingway's most autobiographical characters, Hudson is connected to Montana: "But he had rented the ranch that he owned in Montana because the best time out there was the summer and the fall and now the boys always had to go to school in the fall." Hudson is cast as a painter and his friend Roger Davis is cast as a writer.

Davis struggles with a difficult relationship, a drinking problem, and writer's block. Hemingway headed to the L—T Ranch numerous times throughout the thirties to get his own juices going, so he has Hudson suggest his own ranch as a solution to Roger's problem:

> "Well get the hell out then. Do you want to go to the ranch?"
> "Do you still own it?"
> "Part of it."
> "Is it all right if I go out there."
> "Sure," Thomas Hudson had told him. "But it's rugged from now on until spring and spring isn't easy."
> "I want it to be rugged," Roger had said. "I'm going to start new again."

In Part II, while drowning his sorrows with Honest Lil at the Floridita, mourning in his own way the death of his third son, Hudson remarks on the *highbalito con agua mineral* that Lil is drinking: "That's a fresh water drink. That is the color of Firehole River before it joins the Gibbon to form the Madison." The confluence of the Gibbon and the Firehole rivers (both excellent trout streams) is in Yellowstone National Park. Although Hemingway's many adventures were mostly in the remote region outside of Yellowstone's northeast entrance, he obviously knew the park. He passed through the southern part of the park in 1928 with Pauline on their way home from their first trip out west, camped with John Dos Passos and Floyd Allington "within earshot of a gurgling geyser" at Mammoth Hot Springs in 1930, and signed a menu at the Canyon Lodge in 1957.

In Part III, while chasing Nazis through the Caribbean, Hudson is still haunted by the deaths of his three sons. Just as Robert Jordan reverts back to memories of the Yellowstone High Country during the most pivotal parts of *For Whom the Bell Tolls,* Hudson uses these memories to distract himself from the torment:

> Just lie quiet and watch the night and don't think.
>
>   He was asleep in a little while. He was a boy again and riding up a steep canyon. The canyon opened out and there was a sandbar by the clear river that was so clear he could see pebbles in the bed of the stream and then watch the cutthroat trout at the foot of the pool as they rose to flies that floated down the current. He was sitting on his horse and watching the trout rise when Ara woke him.

[Hudson's orders from Guantanamo interrupt his dream.]

CONTINUE SEARCH CAREFULLY WESTWARD....

He smiled....I have her pretty far west, he thought. I don't think they meant this far west.

True At First Light
1999

True at First Light is a non-fiction account of Hemingway's second and final trip to Africa in the winter of 1953-54. This trip was taken with his fourth wife, Mary Welsh, and ended with two plane crashes and a brush fire, from which he never physically recovered. Around page seventy-eight, Mary expresses to Willie, their affable pilot, her distaste for Hemingway's developing religion: "They all have the same religion now and it's reached a point where it is basically awful. They all eat kipper snacks and drink beer at eleven and explain it is part of their religion....They have horrible slogans and dreadful secrets."

   Hemingway seeks to counter Mary and offer his own explanation to Willie: "We retain the best of various other sects and tribal law and customs. But we weld them into a whole that all can believe. Miss Mary coming from the Northern Frontier Province, Minnesota, and never having been to the Rocky Mountains until we were married is handicapped." Here Hemingway playfully suggests that anyone seeking any philosophical understanding of the world would be handicapped if they had never been to the Rocky Mountains. On the same page he explains where his "religion" started: "the Wind River Range where the religion was first revealed to me and where I had my early visions." The Wind River Range is in Wyoming.

In Chapter 11, Hemingway again uses his experiences in the Yellowstone High Country to separate himself from Mary. While watching eagles and storks feed on the African savannah: "Miss Mary's sorrow resisted the eagles because eagles did not mean as much to me as they did to her.... She had never lain under a juniper bush up above timberline at the top of a pass in our own mountains waiting for eagles to come to a dead horse that had been a bear bait until the bear was killed." From here, the author dedicates three pages to a specific hunt in 1932. There is a careful description of the euthanization of a horse, then the subsequent killing of a bear and an eagle. Then the reader is presented with the image of Hemingway sitting on a mule deer skin in front of a tepee at Lame Deer, Montana, the headquarters of the Northern Cheyenne Indian Reservation, with eagle feathers and bear claws laid out in front of him: "You sat and did not talk and did not talk and sometimes reached out and touched the tails and stroked the plumes very lightly." What was traded for these prizes remains a secret: "I could not tell her what the eagles meant to me... nor what the skins had brought at Lame Deer on the Reservation."

In Chapter 14 Hemingway compares Laitokitok, Kenya, with Cody or Sheridan, Wyoming. In Chapter 19 there is a direct comparison to Cooke City as he shops at a store in the Kenyan town: "...and I liked it because it was like the General Store and Post Office in Cooke City, Montana. In Laitokitok they did not have the cardboard boxes of obsolete calibers that the old-timers bought two to four cartridges from each season in the late fall when they wanted to get their winter meat. They sold spears instead." Even fifteen years after his last trip to Cooke City, Hemingway's thoughts drifted happily back to his time in the Yellowstone High Country. His memory of the Cooke City old-timers buying a couple of bullets in the fall to claim the elk and deer they needed to survive the winter demonstrates an understanding of the area that few "passers through" would be able to claim.

APPENDIX III

Following Papa's Footsteps

Cooke City, Montana

Hemingway mentions Cooke City in *For Whom the Bell Tolls, Across the River and into the Trees* and *True at First Light*. In the preface to *The First Forty-nine Stories* he lists it as one of his favorite places to write along with Paris, Madrid, and Key West. Cooke City is also the setting of Hemingway's final story, "A Man of the World."

Cooke City General Store

Built in 1886 and listed on the National Register of Historic Places, the General Store is the first place to stop on a Hemingway pilgrimage to the area. From this store, Hemingway sent off drafts of *Death in the Afternoon, To Have and Have Not,* the preface to *The First Forty-nine Stories,* and numerous letters. In *True at First Light,* Hemingway reminisces as he shops at a general store in Laitokitok, Kenya: "I liked it because it was like the general store and post office in Cooke City, Montana." The author goes on to explain how the Cooke City shopkeeper would keep almost empty boxes of obsolete calibers of bullets so that old timers with antiquated guns could buy a couple of bullets each fall in order to get their winter meat. As you enter the store, look up and to the right to see some of those old bullet boxes. Being on the National Register of Historic Places, much of the inside of the store remains unchanged from Hemingway's time.

Hoosiers Bar*

Hoosiers opened in 1934 as Prohibition ended. Hemingway visited here in 1936, 1938, and 1939. The first person to tend the bar at Hoosiers was Grace Anderson. She remembered Hemingway coming in the morning or early afternoon, sitting at the end of the bar writing, and pushing his glass forward when he wanted another drink. Hoosiers was open all night, just like the bar in "A Man of the World." This fact, along with other links to Cooke City in the story, means that Hemingway's final story probably takes place at Hoosiers. Cooke City has a population of eighty so it is unlikely that there would be more than one bar open all night. Above the piano in Hoosiers is a picture of the 1930 Old Timers' Fish Fry, and event mentioned in *Across the River and into the Trees.*

> *A cautionary note: Hoosiers is an old-time bar: there is no food, no television, no juke box, no internet, no kids, no pictures, no public restroom, and no patience for people not buying drinks. *Don't ask any Hemingway questions and do not enter unless you plan on having a couple of drinks.*

Yellowstone Trading Post

This gift shop in downtown Cooke City was owned by a man named King Cole in the late thirties. Cooke City historian Ralph Glidden met a relative of Cole's daughter in a hot tub in Arizona and was given a few pages of an unpublished memoir entitled "Memories of Virginia Cole." Within these pages Cole revealed that Hemingway had come in looking for fishing gear in 1939 and his three boys had "tried to steal the whole store."

The Miners Saloon

Built in 1937 as a garage, the Miners is the social hub of Cooke City. It is simply one of the best bars in America and the best place to trade stories or tell lies.

The inside is like a museum and the back bar is a work of art. There is no direct evidence of Hemingway spending time here, but you never know. Stop in regardless for some of the best pizza in the country (really), and the night life.

Beartooth Café

The café was built in 1937 by Lawrence Nordquist, a former owner of the L—T Ranch where Hemingway stayed five times in the 1930s. Hemingway was in the area in 1938 and 1939 so there is a chance he stopped in to see his old friend. There is no direct evidence of such a visit, but it is worth a stop for the smoked trout and the one hundred or so beers on offer.

Silver Gate, Montana

Silver Gate was founded in 1932. With a year-round population less than twenty, this little town sits under Amphitheater Mountain, roughly three miles west of Cooke City and a mile east of Yellowstone's northeast entrance.

The Range Rider Lodge

One of the largest log structures in Montana, the Range Rider was built in 1937 and open for business in 1938 and 1939 for Hemingway's final two visits. Ralph Nelles, who helped build the massive lodge, bartended for those two summers. In his memoir *Village Boy,* Nelles remembers Hemingway coming in every Saturday night for drinks and music. Walking into this stunning lodge is like stepping back in time. The Range Rider has a bar and small rustic rooms that are not much different than in Hemingway's day.

Across from the Range Rider are the *Grizzly Lodge* and the *Log Cabin Café.* Both were built in the thirties and were open for business when Hemingway was coming regularly to Silver Gate.

The Clark's Fork Valley

As you take the winding road east out of Cooke City, the Clark's Fork pours out of the Beartooth Mountains near the Montana-Wyoming border and into the Clark's Fork Valley. The road soon splits into US Highways 296 and 212. Highway 212 (The Beartooth Highway) goes over Beartooth Pass to Red Lodge, Montana. Highway 296 (the Chief Joseph Scenic Byway) goes to Cody, Wyoming. These roads weave in and out of Montana and Wyoming and pass through parts of Custer, Gallatin, and Shoshone national forests and through the Absaroka-Beartooth Wilderness. The following four trails were Hemingway's favorites and are accessible from these roads. Travel with plenty of water, a map, and bear spray.

Pilot Creek Trail

Hemingway had many adventures up this trail including a successful bighorn sheep hunt in 1930, a six-day unsuccessful sheep hunt in 1932, and where he shot a 500-pound black bear in the snow in 1932.

Crazy Creek Trail

Hemingway, Pauline, and John Dos Passos went up this trail to the Crazy Lakes to camp and fish with the Murphy family in 1932. There is a waterfall right at the road and across the valley looms Jim Smith Peak, named after a man whose death was documented in "The Snows of Kilimanjaro."

Granite Lake Trail

Hemingway fished Granite Lake a few times and went there with Pauline, Patrick, and the Shevlins in 1936. Good fishing.

Crandall Creek Trail

Hemingway shot his first bear up Crandall Creek in 1930. About twenty miles up Crandall Creek is *Timber Creek*, possibly Hemingway's favorite hunting terrain, near the Yellowstone border. This area is very rugged and quite dangerous. Bring bear spray and a gun.

Cody, Wyoming

After gashing his leg and face on a hunting trip up Crandall Creek, Hemingway headed to Cody for treatment. After being prescribed a bottle of whiskey, he and Ivan Wallace headed over to an old hotel to drink it. That could have been the Irma Hotel. Across from the Irma sits the *Chamberlain Inn*. Hemingway stayed there on his way out of the Yellowstone High Country in 1932. They have the register he signed on display and a room with Hemingway memorabilia. It is a beautiful boutique hotel with a bar and an outside courtyard. The *Buffalo Bill Museum*, which has one of the world's largest collections of firearms, is also in Cody and worth a visit.

Red Lodge, Montana

Robert Jordan, the hero of *For Whom the Bell Tolls,* is from Red Lodge. After the completion of the Beartooth Highway in 1936, Hemingway would drive to Red Lodge to see his friend Chub Weaver. Before the completion of the highway, the two would ride over on horses. On one of these trips they stopped at Froze-to-Death Lake for Hemingway to drop in the gun his father used to commit suicide. The lake is very hard to get to, take bear spray.

For a slice of history stop at the *Pollard Hotel*, built in 1893. Western legends Buffalo Bill, Calamity Jane, and Liver-eatin' Johnson all stayed there, and Butch Cassidy robbed a bank that used to be in the lobby of the hotel. While we don't know for sure, it is a pretty safe bet that Hemingway wandered in here a few times over the years.

To immerse yourself in Hemingway's Beartooth Mountains, take the trail from East Rosebud Lake (outside of Red Lodge) to Kersey Lake (just outside of Cooke City). Known as *The Beaten Path*, this trail is the preferred backcountry route between the two Montana towns.

Sheridan, Wyoming

Hemingway stayed in and around Sheridan during the summer of 1928. He spent most of his time in the nearby Bighorn Mountains and stayed at the Sheridan Inn for several days while finishing *A Farewell to Arms.* Once owned by Buffalo Bill Cody, this historic hotel is still magnificent and has the old bar, front desk, and dance floor from Hemingway's day. A few blocks from the Sheridan Inn is Val Vista Street. The short story "Wine of Wyoming" was set in an old house with a covered terrace on this street; the exact house is unknown.

Hoosiers Bar in Cooke City in 1934, just after the end of Prohibition. Next to it is the Pilot Café, named after the nearby peak. Hemingway fictionalized both places as the setting for his short story, "A Man of the World."

A Most Interesting Man of the World: Understanding Hemingway's Final Story

by Christopher Warren

As presented at the 2018 International Hemingway Conference, Paris

The history of Hemingway's work in short fiction is easy to follow. There were the 16 stories of *In Our Time* published in 1925, the 14 of *Men Without Women* from 1927, and another 14 in 1933's *Winner Take Nothing*. These 44 stories along with 1923's "Up in Michigan," "The Short Happy Life of Francis Macomber," "The Snows of Kilimanjaro," and "The Capital of the World" all from 1936, and the 1938 story "Old Man at the Bridge" make up *The First Forty-nine Stories* published in 1938. There were then five stories of the Spanish Civil War all published in periodicals in 1938 and 1939. Over the next 22 years Hemingway would publish only four more stories: "The Good Lion" and "The Faithful Bull," two children's stories published in the March 1951 edition of *Holiday* Magazine and finally "Get A Seeing-Eyed Dog" and "A Man of the World" both published in the 100th Anniversary Edition of *The Atlantic Monthly* in December of 1957. These final two stories were published together and "A Man of the World" was actually placed before the other story in the magazine. When we turn to Chapter 74 of Carlos Baker's biography, however, we see that "Get A Seeing-Eyed Dog" was written between 1954 and 1956 and "A Man of the World" was written in 1957, making it Hemingway's final short story.

After its publication in 1957, "A Man of the World" essentially disappeared for 30 years until the release of *The Complete Short Stories: The Finca Vigia Edition* in 1987, leaving a gap in the scholarship. Upon its re-emergence, scholars and students would predictably turn to the Baker biography to provide context. In so doing, they would find this scathing assessment on page 681: "... *he wrote a short story called "A Man of the World," about a malodorous old drunk named Blackie who had been blinded in a tavern brawl in Jessup, Wyoming. "I think it is a good story," Ernest said. If he really thought so, his judgment was slipping."* Here Baker steps out of his role as biographer and into the role of critic. While Hemingway wrote some masterful novels he had some that missed with both critics and audiences, the same can be said of his non-fiction and his only attempts at poetry and playwriting were essentially lacking; his work in short fiction however, is virtually unblemished and given that he, himself considered it a good story, and that it was the final short story of his career, "A Man of the World" deserves a closer look.

Baker's main mistake was to assume that the story is set in Jessup, Wyoming. While the story is set in a town called Jessup there is no mention of Wyoming. Some scholars such as Julian Smith in his essay "Eyeless in Wyoming, Blind in Venice -- Hemingway's Last Stories" have followed Baker down this erroneous path. Howard L. Hannum in his work "Hemingway's 'Tales of the Real Dark'" suggests that character Willie Sawyer's last name connects the story to the Sawtooth Mountains outside of Ketchum, Idaho, while Charles Oliver in "A to Z: The Essential Reference to the Life and Work" lists Jessup as an "otherwise unidentified western U.S. Town." This confusion as to the setting of Hemingway's final story is indicative of the scholarship's misunderstanding of the author's time in the American West. As the bulk of Hemingway's fiction is based on actual events, people and places, it is always important to uncover the actual inspiration for the work. When we understand that the actual inspiration for Jessup is Cooke City, Montana, we can better understand the story's place in Hemingway's fiction.

The action in "A Man of the World" takes place in two bars: one called 'The Pilot' and one called 'The Index.' Pilot and Index are two mountains connected by a short saddle on the Montana-Wyoming border that are always referred to together. Throughout the thirties while at the L—T Ranch, Hemingway would wake to a spectacular view of the two peaks. He had intimate knowledge of the mountains having shot the only bighorn sheep of his life on their slopes in 1930 and the biggest black bear of his life at the foot of great mountains in 1932. He remembered them this way in a 1939 essay for *Vogue:*

> *Up the river were the two peaks of Pilot and Index, where we would hunt mountain-sheep later in the month, and you sat in the sun and marveled at the formal, clean-lined shape mountains can have at a distance, so that you remember them in the shapes they show from far away, and not as the broken rockslides you crossed and jagged edges you pulled up by, and the narrow shelves you sweated along, afraid to look down, to round that peak that looked so smooth and geometrical.*

There is only one town within 60 miles of Pilot and Index; that town is Cooke City, Montana. Scholars should already be familiar with Cooke City; Hemingway mentioned it in the Preface to *The First Forty-nine Stories* as one of his favorite places to write, behind only Paris, Madrid and Key West. He had written about Cooke City in *For Whom the Bell Tolls, Across the River and into the Trees* and *True at First Light* and had also sent off final drafts of *Death in the Afternoon* and *To Have and Have Not* from the Cooke City General Store.

There are several things in "A Man of the World" that reveal Jessup as simply a pseudonym for the Montana town: When protagonist "Blindie" mentions having to be careful on "those roads" he is immediately corrected: "*What do you mean those roads? You only go on one road.*" For six months of the year there is one road that comes in to Cooke and the same road goes out. In winter, however, the road out of Cooke City is closed due to snow, meaning there is literally only one road in.

The main event in the story is a barroom fight, and Frank, the bartender, describes the brawl as happening "*on the ice of the road with snow all banked up and the light from this door and The Index door.*" To anyone who has wintered in Cooke City over the last 100 or so years this will be a familiar image. Cooke averages 500 inches of snow annually, as the year progresses, snow piles up along the road and around the buildings. Fights usually start in the bars and spill out into the street. As Blindie enters the bar he "*has icicles on his mustache and small pus icicles out of both eyes"* – Cooke City sits at almost 8,000 feet and 20 below zero is common; residents usually see 40 below zero at least once a year. When it is this cold, beards and mustaches freeze.

The most telling evidence that "A Man of the World" is set in Cooke City, Montana, comes when we compare Hemingway's description of the bar "The Index" to the memories of local resident Grace Anderson and her description of Hoosiers Bar in the 1930s. In the second paragraph of "A Man of the World" Hemingway describes The Index: *"Then The Index was open all night long and got the early morning trade."* In a 1970 interview with Addison Bragg of the *Billings Gazette*, Grace Anderson who worked at Hoosiers Bar in the thirties (her picture is still up next to the door) remembered Hemingway coming in in the mornings: "We never closed... He'd sit at the end of the bar and push his glass across the bar when he wanted another drink." Finally when we look at this picture of Hoosiers Bar from 1934 we notice the little place next to it is called the Pilot Café.

So we have a bar—Hoosiers—that is in a town Hemingway wrote about, one that he patronized in the mornings, one that was open all night, and one that is next to a place called the Pilot Café. Then we have The Index of "A Man of the World" which got "the early morning trade," "was open all night long" and was right next to a place called the The Pilot. This evidence establishes Cooke City, Montana, as the setting for Hemingway's last story and even identifies Hoosiers as one of the bars in which the story takes place.

With Cooke City as the established setting, we can begin assess what seems to be over-the-top violence at the center of the story. The story's plot revolves around a fight remembered by the patrons of a bar on a cold winter night similar to the one on which the fight took place. The combatants Willie Sawyer and Blackie both suffer grievous injuries; Blackie has both his eyes gouged out and then has his genitals stomped, causing a scream that blows out his vocal chords. Sawyer ends up with a hole in his face from a bite from Blackie. This is far from the macho, stand up type of boxing match that Hemingway might have preferred, but in a depressed mining town in midwinter, a "to the death battle" such as the one described is a little easier to imagine. When we realize that the nearest police presence remains two hours away to this day the notion of things getting out of hand is also easy to accept.

When we look at the violent history from this region, detailed in Ed Spencer's *A History (more or less) of the RDS, B—4, L—T and Hancock Ranches,* as well as Hemingway's own memories of the place we begin to see how the gruesome story was conceived. Cooke City sits ten miles to the west of the L—T Ranch where Hemingway stayed for the summer in 1930, '32, '36, '38 and '39. The original homesteader of the L—T was a man named Jim Smith. Smith was shot and killed by a ranch hand in a dispute over hay in 1912. We know Hemingway knew of Smith's murder because he describes it in detail during one of the hallucinatory passages toward the end of "The Snows of Kilimanjaro." The killing was eventually ruled "justifiable homicide" by a judge in Cody, Wyoming. Jim Smith Peak towers above the L—T, just east of Cooke City.

Many of Hemingway's greatest hunting exploits in the American West took place up Crandall Creek. Crandall is where he would shoot his first bear in 1930, several elk in '30,'32 and '36 and the only grizzly of his life also in 1936. Crandall Creek is named after Jack Crandall, a prospector who was killed along with his partner at their camp. While the killings were blamed on Crow Indians in the region, it was generally understood that the two men were murdered by rival prospectors since their heads were severed and impaled on their pick-axes, in front of their tent.

Between Hemingway's second and third visits to the ranch, there was another high-profile example of extreme violence involving Budd Hart, a prospector and stonemason who had built the stone fireplace at the L—T. Late on the night of September 1, 1935, two men kicked in the door of Hart's cabin on the east edge of Cooke City. "We're taking you for a ride," shouted one of the men. Hart pulled a pistol from under his pillow and shot the first attacker, killing him. When his gun jammed, Hart grabbed an axe and quickly dispatched the second man. The arrest, indictment, and trial that followed in Livingston, Montana, over the next few weeks were front-page news in the *Livingston Enterprise.* The source of the large wads of cash the two men showed at the bar, where they fortified their courage before going to Hart's cabin, was never identified. But after a week-long trial, including all the gory details, it took the jury of 12 men less than an hour to rule that Hart had acted in self-defense. By the time Hemingway arrived in Cooke City the following summer, the acquittal was long forgotten but the murders were entrenched local lore, with the violence and mayhem embellished at each retelling.

After breaking his arm in 1930, Hemingway spent seven weeks at St. Vincent's Hospital in Billings. While there, he shared space with the victims of a gunfight that occurred during a poker game.

There is one more, dark tale of violence that Hemingway wrote about in a piece called "A Paris Letter" published by *Esquire* in February of 1934. Hemingway begins:

"This time last year we were driving home from Cooke City, Montana, in a blizzard. The boys who had tried to drag Bull Neck Moose Face, the truck driver, to death the night of the Old Timers Fish Fry because he was alleged to have hit a woman with a poker, were still in jail.

It was events such as these that inspired Hemingway, through the voice of Colonel Cantwell of *Across the River and into the Trees,* to use Cooke City as the standard of what constitutes a tough town:

"O.K., Jackson. Maybe we move in different circles. Or maybe we have a differing definition for the word. But this town of Venice, with everybody being polite and having good manners, is as tough as Cooke City, Montana, on the day they have the Old Timers' Fish Fry.

With the setting established, the culture of violence, along with Hemingway's understanding of it, explained, Blindie can take his place among other characters in the fiction. What makes Blindie a "man of the world" is his stoicism in the face of adversity. Like Ole Andersson in "The Killers," Blindie refuses to condemn his attacker. He is related most closely, however, to another character from Hemingway's short stories. "The Gambler, the Nun, and the Radio" tells the story of Hemingway's recuperation in a Billings Hospital from a broken arm he suffered while driving out of Cooke City in 1930. The story begins with the biographical protagonist, Mr. Frazier, translating for a "Mexican" named Cayetano, who has been shot twice during a card game and is now being interrogated by a detective. As the detective presses him to reveal his attacker, Cayetano refuses, saying he was shot in the back and didn't see him. Later in the story he explains that he was shot twice "in the belly" revealing that he knew exactly who shot him but would not expose or denounce him. When it becomes apparent that Cayetano will lose the use of his leg he remarks cheerfully, "I have no use for the leg. I am all right with the leg or not." Blindie, of "A Man of the World," has had both his eyes gouged out and his genitals stomped by Willie Sawyer. Though he has been blinded, silenced and potentially neutered, Blindie's only complaint about Willie Sawyer is that he has no sense of humor. Like Cayetano, he has accepted his new role in the world and the limits the altercation has put upon him. Both stories are set in Montana, and both stories address how men deal with injury.

Hemingway's obsession with injury and recovery permeates his work. Many of the injuries his characters have to endure are based on his own. Just as the predicaments in which Frederick Henry and Jake Barnes find themselves relate directly to Hemingway's injury during WWI, and the injuries Harry Morgan and Robert Jordan sustain during the climax of their respective novels are influenced by the broken arm he suffered while leaving Cooke City in 1930, so too are Blindie's injuries directly related to the predicament the author found himself in toward the end of his life. Surely having his eyes gouged out would have been enough for Blindie to join Hemingway's legion of wounded characters. Why then the stomping of the genitals and the subsequent loss of voice. This gratuitousness is another thing that has bothered critics about this story.

In my opinion, developed through my research for this book, Blindie has to suffer these specific injuries in order to reflect the way Hemingway saw himself towards the end of his life. The blindness mirrors the author's well-documented struggles with his eyesight. Selma Karayalcin points out in her essay "Hemingway's Fishing Rod" that upon his return trip to Africa in 1954, his historically poor vision was beginning to fail, as he was unable to hit standing game with any accuracy. The compromised voice reflects Hemingway's inability to write effectively in his final years. "Across the River and into the Trees" was not well received and neither were his final four stories, including this one. The genital stomping echoes the sexual inadequacy that inhabits so many Hemingway characters as illustrated by Mark Cirino and Amanda Kay Oaks in their essay "Wise Blood." The cruel castration also corresponds to the impotency the writer had struggled with since his mid-forties. Being in his late fifties and approaching the end of a life of injury and alcoholism, it is easy to see this problem resurfacing.

It is no secret that Dos Equis' "Most Interesting Man in the World" ad campaign is based on Hemingway and it was no accident that Hemingway's final story is called "A Man of the World." Both are caricatures of Hemingway: one, the comedic worldview offered up by pop culture, the other is the nuanced, if grotesque view of the author offered by Hemingway himself. Just as Nick, his first fictional character is introduced to the world through violence and darkness in "Indian Camp," his final fictional character exits the same way. Like Hemingway himself, "Blindie" is left blind, voiceless and impotent by a world that doesn't care. This is the naturalist crux of Hemingway's fiction: Frederick Henry will not live happily ever after, Jake Barnes will not get the girl, Robert Jordan will not ride off into the sunset, and Santiago will not get that marlin back to the village. Blindie, as malodorous as he may be, understands and even cheerfully accepts this and that is what makes him a perfect example of the Hemingway code hero and in turn "A Man of the World."

Endnotes

Introduction

1. Ralph Glidden, personal interviews.

2. Tom Weaver, personal interviews.

3. Sue Hart, "Writing the West: Hemingway, Fishing and Friends at the L—T." (*Big Sky Journal*, Fly Fishing Edition, 2006).

4. *Atlantic Monthly,* 100th anniversary edition, 1957.

5. Howard L. Hamman, *Hemingway's Tales of the Real Dark.*

6. Charles M. Oliver, *Hemingway A to Z: The Essential Reference to the Life and Work.* (New York: Facts on File, 1999).

7. Ernest Hemingway, *The Complete Short Stories of Ernest Hemingway: The Finca Vigía Edition.* (New York: Charles Scribner's Sons, 1987).

8. Jeffrey Myers, *Hemingway: A Biography.* (New York: Harper and Row, 1985), 223.

9. *For Whom the Bell Tolls,* Chapter 30.

10. *Ernest Hemingway, Selected Letters, 1917-1961.* (New York: Charles Scribner's Sons, 1981) Letter to Perkins 7-27-1932.

11. Ralph Glidden, *Exploring the Yellowstone High Country: A History of the Cooke City Area.* (Cooke City: Cooke City Community Council, 1976).

12. Lee Alan Gutkind, articles in the *Des Moines Register,* 1970.

13. Ibid.

14. Ed Spenser and K. T. Roes, *A History (more or less) of the RDS, B-4, L-T and Hancock Ranches.* (Cody, Wyoming: Wordsworth Publishing, 2004), 13.

15. Carlos Baker, *Ernest Hemingway: A Life Story.* (New York: Charles Scribner's Sons, 1969), 271.

16. Michael, Reynolds, *Hemingway: The 1930s.* (New York: W.W. Norton & Company, 1997), 44.

17. Spenser, *A History,* 12.

18. Baker, *Ernest Hemingway,* 272.

19. Dink Bruce, personal interviews.

Chapter I 1928

1. Baker, *Ernest Hemingway*, 250.

2. Ibid., 251.

3. Hemingway, *Selected Letters,* Letter to Guy Hickok 7-27-28.

4. Bill Horne, interview (*Barrington Courier Review,* September 27, 1979), 30.

5. Hemingway, *Selected Letters,* Letter to Waldo Pierce, 282.

6. Horne, *Barrington*, 30.

7. Hemingway, *Selected Letters*, 282.

8. Lee Alan Gutkind, "Hemingway in Wyoming." (*Casper Star Tribune*, October 17, 1970), 9.

9. Ernest Hemingway, *The Letters of Ernest Hemingway: Volume 3 (1926-1929).* (New York: Cambridge University Press, 2015), 422.

10. Baker, *Ernest Hemingway,* 257.

Chapter II 1930

1. Baker, *Ernest Hemingway,* 271.

2. Myers, *Hemingway*, 223.

3. Spencer, *A History*, 12.

4. Ernest Hemingway, *The Only Thing That Counts: The Ernest Hemingway-Maxwell Perkins Correspondence 1925- 1947.* (New York: Scribner, 1996), 145-146.

5. Lea H. Lawrence, *Prowling Papa's Waters.* (Marietta, Georgia: Long Street Press Inc. 1992), 176.

6. Baker, *Ernest Hemingway,* 272.

7. Sue Hart, "Writing the West: Hemingway, fishing and friends at the L-T Ranch." (*Big Sky Journal*, Fly Fishing Edition, 2006), 65.

8. Ernest Hemingway, *Hemingway on Fishing. (*New York: Scribner, 2000), xi.

9. Jack Hemingway, *Misadventures of a Fly Fisherman: My Life With and Without Papa.* (New York: McGraw-Hill, 1987), 109.

10. Glidden, *Exploring.*

11. Baker, *Ernest Hemingway*, 274.

12. Gutkind, *Des Moines Register.*

13. Hemingway, *Selected Letters*, 328.

14. Ernest Hemingway, "The Clark's Fork Valley, Wyoming." (*Vogue*, February 1939).

15. Hemingway, *Selected Letters*, 371.

16. Baker, *Ernest Hemingway,* 276.

17. Ernest Hemingway, *Green Hills of Africa* (New York: Charles Scribner's Sons, 1935), 54.

18. Hemingway, "The Clark's Fork Valley."

19. Baker, *Ernest Hemingway*, 277.

20. Ibid.

21. Hart, "Writing the West," 68.

22. Hemingway, *Green Hills,* 147-148.

23. Myers, *Hemingway*, 223.

24. Hart, "Writing the West," 70.

25. Dink Bruce, personal interviews.

26. Baker, *Ernest Hemingway*, 223.

Chapter III 1932

1. Reynolds, *Hemingway,* 64.

2. Denis Brian, *The True Gen: An Intimate Portrait of Ernest Hemingway by Those Who Knew Him.* (New York: Grove Press, 1988.) 295.

3. Reynolds, *Hemingway,* 97.

4. Hart, "Writing the West," 67.

5. Brian, *The True Gen*, 82.

6. Ibid.

7. Hart, "Writing the West," 65.

8. Patrick Hemingway, interview, "Paradise and Purgatory: Hemingway of The L Bar T and St. V's." Montana PBS, 2017.

9. Honoria Murphy Donnelly, *Sara and Gerald: Villa America and After.* (New York: Times Books, 1982.), 67.

10. Ibid., 68.

11. Paul Hendrickson, *Hemingway's Boat: Everything He Loved in Life, and Lost, 1934-1961.* (London: Bodley Head, 2012.), 241-242.

12. Hemingway, *Selected Letters,* 371.

13. Ibid., 372.

14. Baker, *Ernest Hemingway*, 298.

15. Hemingway, *Selected Letters*, 364.

16. Ibid., 365.

17. Hemingway, *The Only,* 176.

18. Hemingway, *Selected Letters,* 367.

19. Ernest Hemingway, "Homage to Switzerland."

20. Hemingway, *Selected Letters,* 365.

21. Ibid., 368.

22. Baker, *Ernest Hemingway,* 298.

23. Hemingway, *Selected Letters,* 369.

24. Pilot Peak FA, 1932 Youtube.

25. Baker, *Ernest Hemingway,* 299.

26. Hemingway, *Selected Letters,* 371.

27. Gregory Hemingway, *Papa: A Personal Memoir.* (Boston: Houghton Mifflin, 1976.) 56-57.

28. Hemingway, Selected Letters, 372.

29. Ibid., 373-374.

30. Baker, *Ernest Hemingway,* 297.

31. Reynolds, *Hemingway,* 102.
32. Hotel register, Chamberlin Inn (formerly Chamberlin Hotel).

Chapter IV 1936

1. Baker, *Ernest Hemingway,* 372.
2. Spencer, *A History,* 13.
3. Reynolds, *Hemingway,* 235.
4. Patrick Hemingway, interview, "Paradise and Purgatory," Montana PBS.
5. Hemingway, *Selected Letters,* 451.
6. Ernest Hemingway, "Fathers and Sons."
7. Ernest Hemingway, "The Snows of Kilimanjaro."
8. Spencer, *A History,* 8.
9. Hemingway, *Selected Letters,* 454-455.
10. Baker, *Ernest Hemingway,* 373.
11. Baker, *Ernest Hemingway,* 830.
12. Hemingway, *Selected Letters,* 454.
13. A. E. Hotchner, *The Good Life According to Ernest Hemingway.* (New York: HarperCollins, 2008.) 73.
14. Hemingway, *Selected Letters,* 451.
15. Baker, *Ernest Hemingway,* 374.
16. Hemingway, *Selected Letters,* 453.
17. Brian, *True Gen,* 98.
18. Hemingway, *Selected Letters,* 449.
19. Baker, *Ernest Hemingway,* 377.
20. Hart, "Writing the West," 66.
21. Ernest Hemingway, "A Man of the World," *Atlantic Monthly,* centennial edition, 1957.
22. Jon Fryer, personal interview.

Chapter V 1938

1. Spencer, *A History,* 13.
2. Hemingway, *Selected Letters,* 375.
3. *Life* Magazine, July 12, 1937, 19.
4. Baker, *Ernest Hemingway,* 399.
5. Hemingway, *The Only,* 268.
6. Ernest Hemingway, *The Fifth Column and the First Forty-nine Stories.* (New York: Charles Scribner's Sons, 1938).
7. Ibid.
8. Spencer, *A History,* 13.
9. Baker, *Ernest Hemingway,* 423.

10. Ibid., 424.

11. Spencer, *A History*, 14.

12. Ibid., 14.

13. Nelles, *Village Boy*, 25.

14. Hemingway, *Selected Letters,* 473.

15. Baker, *Ernest Hemingway*, 428-29.

16. Ernest Hemingway, *For Whom the Bell Tolls.* (New York: Charles Scribner's Sons, 1940) 438.

17. Ibid., 448.

18. Ibid., 460-461.

19. Ibid., 461.

20. Hemingway, *Selected Letters,* 334.

21. Hemingway, *For Whom,* 470.

22. Ibid., 471.

23. Baker, *Ernest Hemingway*, 432.

Chapter VI 1939

1. Hemingway, *Selected Letters*, 488.

2. Ibid., 489.

3. Ibid., 492.

4. Ibid., 491.

5. Ibid.

6. Hemingway, *For Whom,* 337.

7. Hart, "Writing the West," and Tom Weaver, personal interviews.

8. Hemingway, *Selected Letters,* 496.

9. Hemingway, "The Clark's Fork Valley," *Vogue* Magazine, February 1939, 157.

10. William Kittredge, *The Portable Western Reader.* (New York: Penguin Books, 1997).

11. Baker, *Ernest Hemingway*, 433.

12. Spencer, *A History*, 14.

13. Ibid., 14.

14. Hemingway, *For Whom,* 337.

15. Spencer, *A History*, 14.

16. Hemingway, *Selected Letters,* 499.

Chapter VII After he left

1. Jack Hemingway, *Hemingway on Fishing,* xi.

2. Baker, *Ernest Hemingway*, 447.

3. Baker, *Ernest Hemingway*, 712.

4. Hart, "Writing the West," 64.

Bibliography

Baker, Carlos. *Ernest Hemingway: A Life Story*. New York: Charles Scribner's Sons, 1969.

Bragg, Addison. "In the Legend." *Billings Gazette*, November 15, 1970.

Brian, Denis. *The True Gen: An Intimate Portrait of Ernest Hemingway by Those Who Knew Him*. New York: Grove Press, 1988.

Bruce, Dink. Personal interviews.

Cole, Virginia. Personal memories presented to Ralph Glidden, Cooke City, Montana.

Dearborn, Mary V. *Ernest Hemingway: A Biography*. New York: Knopf, 2017.

Donnelly, Honoria Murphy. *Sara and Gerald: Villa America and After*. New York: Times Books, 1982.

Fryer, Jon. Personal interview.

Glidden, Ralph. *Exploring the Yellowstone High Country: A History of the Cooke City Area*. Cooke City: Cooke City Community Council, 1976.

Glidden, Ralph. Personal interviews.

Gutkind, Alan Lee. "Hemingway in Wyoming." *Casper Star Tribune*, September-October, 1970.

Hemingway, Ernest

    A Farewell to Arms. New York: Charles Scribner's Sons, 1929.

    Across the River and into the Trees. New York: Charles Scribner's Sons, 1950.

    By-line: Ernest Hemingway; Selected Articles and Dispatches of Four Decades. Edited by William White. New York: Charles Scribner's Sons, 1967.

    Death in the Afternoon. New York: Charles Scribner's Sons, 1932.

    Ernest Hemingway, Selected Letters, 1917-1961. Edited by Carlos Baker. New York: Charles Scribner's Sons, 1981.

    For Whom the Bell Tolls. New York: Charles Scribner's Sons, 1940.

    Green Hills of Africa. New York: Charles Scribner's Sons, 1935.

    Hemingway on Fishing. Edited by Nick Lyons, New York: Scribner, 2000.

    Islands in the Stream. New York: Charles Scribner's Sons, 1970.

    Men Without Women. New York: Charles Scribner's Sons, 1927.

The Fifth Column and the First Forty-nine Stories. New York: Charles Scribner's Sons, 1938.

The Nick Adams Stories. New York: Charles Scribner's Sons, 1972.

"The Clark's Fork Valley, Wyoming." In *The Portable Western Reader.* Edited by William Kittredge. New York: Penguin Books, 1997.

The Complete Short Stories of Ernest Hemingway: The Finca Vigía Edition. New York: Charles Scribner's Sons, 1987.

The Letters of Ernest Hemingway: Volume 3 (1926-1929). Edited by Rena Sanderson, Sandra Spanier, and Robert W. Trogdon. New York: Cambridge University Press, 2015.

The Old Man and the Sea. New York: Charles Scribner's Sons, 1952.

The Only Thing That Counts: The Ernest Hemingway-Maxwell Perkins Correspondence 1925- 1947. Edited by Matthew J. Bruccoli. New York: Scribner, 1996.

The Sun Also Rises. New York: Charles Scribner's Sons, 1926.

To Have and Have Not. New York: Charles Scribner's Sons, 1937.

True at First Light. Edited by Patrick Hemingway. New York: Charles Scribner's Sons, 1999.

Winner Take Nothing. New York: Charles Scribner's Sons, 1933.

Hemingway, Gregory. *Papa: A Personal Memoir.* Boston: Houghton Mifflin, 1976.

Hemingway, Jack. *Misadventures of a Fly Fisherman: My Life With and Without Papa.* New York: Mc-Graw-Hill, 1987.

Hart, Sue. "Writing the West: Hemingway, fishing and friends at the L-T Ranch." *Big Sky Journal,* Fly Fishing Edition, 2006.

Hendrickson, Paul. *Hemingway's Boat: Everything He Loved in Life, and Lost, 1934-1961.* London: Bodley Head, 2012.

Hoskins, Robert. "Paradise Lost." *Wyoming Wildlife,* January 1997.

Hotchner, A. E. *The Good Life According to Ernest Hemingway.* New York: HarperCollins, 2008.

Lawrence, H. Lea. *Prowling Papa's Waters.* Marietta, Georgia: Long Street Press Inc. 1992.

"Letter" from occupants of the L—T Ranch to Ernest Hemingway in 1931, provided by Dink Bruce.

Moseley, Virginia K. "Hemingway and Horne – friends from the front." *Barrington Courier Review,* September 27, 1979.

Myers, Jeffrey. *Hemingway: A Biography.* New York: Harper and Row, 1985

Nelles, Ralph. *Village Boy.* Self-published, 2003.

Oliver, Charles M. *Ernest Hemingway A to Z: The Essential Reference to the Life and Work.* New York: Facts on File, 1999.

"Paradise and Purgatory: Hemingway of The L Bar T and St. V's." Montana PBS, 2017.

Reynolds, Michael. *Hemingway: The 1930s.* New York: W.W. Norton & Company, 1997.

Sheridan County Fulmer Public Library, *Ernest Hemingway – His 1928 Stay in the Bighorn Mountains of Wyoming.* THE Wyoming Room, Sheridan County Fulmer Public Library.

Spenser, Ed, and Roes, K.T. *A History (more or less) of the RDS, B-4, L-T and Hancock Ranches.* Cody, Wyoming: Wordsworth Publishing, 2004.

Weaver, Tom. Personal interviews.

Index

Works by Ernest Hemingway

People, other than Ernest Hemingway

Places and Things